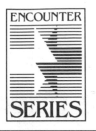

ENCOUNTER
SERIES

The Preferential Option for the Poor

Essays by

Robert Benne
Dennis P. McCann
Gilbert Meilaender
Max L. Stackhouse

and
The Story of an Encounter by
David Heim

Edited and with a Foreword by
Richard John Neuhaus

WILLIAM B. EERDMANS PUBLISHING COMPANY
GRAND RAPIDS, MICHIGAN

Published by Wm. B. Eerdmans Publishing Co.
in cooperation with
The Rockford Institute Center on Religion & Society

Library of Congress Cataloging-in-Publication Data

The Preferential option for the poor: essays / by Max L. Stackhouse
... [et al.] and The story of an encounter by David Heim; edited
and with a foreword by Richard John Neuhaus.
    p.   cm.   — (The Encounter series; 8)
    ISBN 0-8028-0208-7
    1. Church work with the poor—Congresses. 2. Poverty—Religious
aspects—Christianity—Congresses. I. Stackhouse, Max L.
II. Neuhaus, Richard John. III. Series: Encounter series (Grand
Rapids, Mich.); 8.
BV639.P6P73 1988
261.8'3456—dc19   88-10201
                                      CIP

Contents

Foreword

Today's sensitivities about "truth in advertising" would seem to require a warning about this book. The arguments and contentions in these pages are not only lively, they are frequently heated. In addition, this book does not come with any assurances such as "satisfaction guaranteed." On the contrary, I fully expect that many readers will be both unsatisfied and dissatisfied. I know I am.

Despite that, this is a great book, and you should read it. I will go further and say you should read it because of that. What makes it a great book, in my judgment, is that it unsettles a cluster of too-settled ideas that have attached themselves to the phrase "preferential option for the poor." In many circles today, the very utterance of the phrase is almost certain to spark predictable and polarized responses. The "preferential option for the poor" has in recent years been pressed most vigorously in varieties of Liberation Theology. Yet the idea that the poor have a special place in God's purposes in history is hardly an insight produced by the last ten or twenty years. Nor does one have to leap back over the centuries in order to discover the insight in "Bible politics." As Max Stackhouse's essay on Protestant thought makes clear, the puzzlement about the poor in providential purpose has been a staple in Christian mulling about the meaning of justice.

Stackhouse, Benne, McCann, and Meilaender do not by any means emerge from this puzzlement with the same conclusions. The four essayists are each moral theologians of one sort or another, but a glance at the list of those who participated in the conference that gave rise to this volume alerts the reader to the fact that the theology and ethics of the essayists are challenged by practitioners and thinkers whose everyday work is more focused on policy specifics than on general principle. In the conference, policies and principles were in deepest conversation, being raised against one another, being held accountable to one another. Again and again, participants said they had seldom experienced anything like it. Some of the tensions and delights of that conversation come through in David Heim's "Story of an Encounter."

The book also tries to be specific when it comes to the poor in question. "The poor" is not an ideological category; it is a multitude of very real people, people who are almost inescapable in our cities and countryside (though it is no secret that many Americans would dearly love to escape them). Domestic poverty comes in for the most intense examination. Never far from the minds of the participants was the phenomenon described as the "new underclass" in American life, composed notably, but not exclusively, of the urban and the black. The reader will encounter some of the most promising rethinking that is going on in black America, represented by participants such as Glenn Loury and Robert Woodson.

The thinking and rethinking, as you might expect, has much to do with the swamp of policies, discontents, disappointments, and disasters that are to be found in the general category of "welfare policy." In 1987 the news media paid a great deal of attention to the "new consensus" that presumably had emerged on welfare policy. In this case the attention cannot be dismissed as media hype. Reflecting this development was a study entitled *The New Consensus on Family and Welfare*, published by Marquette University (Milwaukee) and the American Enterprise Institute (Washington, D.C.). That study is playing a key role in the wrestling of federal and state governments with "welfare reform," and some of the key actors in that study were engaged in the conference that produced this book. The singular thing about this book is that we see these policy actors making themselves vulnerable to the philosophical, moral, and even theological presuppositions that shape our thinking about "the poor"—our responsibility for them, our relationship with them.

For any reader of this book, the poor are almost certainly "them." They are, for the most part, at a distance. We need to get up closer. The "them" needs to be, as some participants put it, "disaggregated" into specific individuals, communities, patterns of behavior, disabilities and strengths. The poor are neither the salvific agents of human liberation that some portray them to be, nor, as others would have it, are they the bothersome refuse that the rest of us must grudgingly tolerate and minimally support. They share with all of us what some of us persist in calling a human nature, which is, among other things, a way of being that is marked by virtues and vices that have the most direct bearing on the part we play in society.

Twenty years after the exuberant hopes associated with the Great Society, it is widely recognized that wars on poverty have too often turned into wars on the poor. The syndrome of "welfare dependency" is now almost universally recognized and deplored. And, if the truth be told, many Americans are simply sick and tired of being scolded about the poor and what we should do for them and about them. While sympathetically understanding why people have wearied of the subject, this volume makes clear why the questions will not go away. More important, it poses old questions in new ways and introduces the reader to the different and more promising responses that are being advanced today. That said, satisfaction with this book is still not guaranteed. While the publisher is not quite prepared to offer a money-back guarantee, we do think he would be on safe ground in making the promise that, after this book, readers will not think about "the poor" in the way they did before.

The Rockford Institute Center on Religion & Society is indebted to The Pew Charitable Trusts for financial assistance with the conference, and I am thankful once again to my colleagues Allan Carlson, Paul Stallsworth, and Davida Goldman, who make these things work so remarkably well.

Richard John Neuhaus

THE ROCKFORD INSTITUTE
CENTER ON RELIGION & SOCIETY
NEW YORK CITY

Protestantism and Poverty

Max L. Stackhouse

WHY THE TOPIC?

Every effort to understand the past is undertaken to help the present face the future. We study previous chapters in history to find the roots of those influences that have made us what we are and made modernity what it is. We exhume the dead to discover the perennial structures of life. We recover neglected insights of sages long forgotten (or distorted) to deprovincialize the perspectives of our little heres and nows. We trace trajectories that seem to press from ages past through the present to the destinies of tomorrow so that we can wrestle with probabilities with which we must contend. More frequently than not, the motives for investigating any history are both "scientific" and ethical. We investigate; we also evaluate. Fact is joined to value in history, and yet they are not the same. We want to know what happened, and thus we apply the canons of descriptive accuracy; we want to assess, and so we seek normative principles to judge what happened, is happening, and might well happen.

The request that I prepare a paper on "the Protestant tradition with respect to the question of accountability to the poor," and that it "should be historical, of course," is without question rooted in such a mixture of motivations. Indeed, I was instructed that I should not feel myself "limited in any way to past and present." In fact, wrote Pastor Neuhaus, "we . . . will be exploring the possible futures of the question at hand."

Such concerns are not entirely new in twentieth-century Protestantism. They have been among the recurrent themes of the ecumenical movement. In 1910 the World Missionary Conference brought representatives of the Protestant churches from around the globe together in Edinburgh and established the major "instrumentalities" that, after World War II, were to become the core of the World Council of Churches. That conference marked the convergence of the major branches of Protestantism after centuries of growing divergence. And they made clear that one of the points on which modern Protestantism would be tested would be its capacity to speak creatively from its traditions to newer perspectives brought by rapid industrialization in the age of "progress."

Already, it had been recognized that a new cooperative spirit was demanded to mend the torn garment of Christ *and* face the distinctive challenges of the modern age. The relationship of Protestant theology to economic questions, the "rationalization" of production, the colonialization of the Third World, and the urbanization of life were bursting the constraints of traditional economies, displacing farmers, producing new classes of workers, allowing the rise of the robber barons, and forming new underclasses. The possessive individualism of Adam Smith had already long prompted *homo economicus* to sever business and its "dismal science" from *homo religiosis*. Already "the specter of Communism," as Karl Marx called it, was beginning to haunt the world. Already the Roman Catholic social encyclicals were condemning modernity and opening the door to new socioeconomic criticism on theological grounds. Already fundamentalists had begun to cut themselves off from the Protestant mainstream that embraced the dialogue of religion and modern science. Already protoecumenical Protestants had entered into the war against slavery, founded settlement houses, fomented the creation of labor unions, and established the new discipline of Christian social ethics. Many felt that the confessional and ecclesiological points that had split the Reformation heritage into a hundred pieces were less important than basic attitudes toward social questions.[1]

In Europe the Evangelical Social Congress had already been formed to produce a "non-Communist Internationale," fascinated by the possibilities of a non-Marxist Christian Socialism. In the United States, the Social Gospel had been brewing for half a century when the newly formed Federal Council of Churches of Christ in America passed, in 1908, its first major pronouncement, "The Church and Modern Industry."[2] Ecumenically oriented Protes-

---

1. See my *Public Theology and Political Economy* (Grand Rapids: Eerdmans, 1987); and *The Bible in American Law, Politics, and Political Rhetoric,* ed. James T. Johnson (Philadelphia: Fortress Press, 1985).

2. The text of this document can be found in my *Creeds, Society, and Human Rights: A Study in Three Cultures* (Grand Rapids: Eerdmans, 1984), pp. 290-94. See also William O. Shanahan, *German Protestants Face the Social Question* (Notre Dame, Ind.: University of Notre Dame Press, 1954); Alfred Dudley Ward, *The Social Creed of the Methodist Church: A Living Document* (Nashville: Abingdon Press, 1961); Paul Bock, *In Search of a Re-*

tantism had already wrestled with Smith and Marx and determined them both to be un-Christian, deficient in understanding how religion and economics interacted in social history, and inadequate even as "scientific" analysts of how modern social economies work.[3] And Max Weber had already published his controversial work *The Protestant Ethic and the Spirit of Capitalism*, beginning a debate not yet ended.

Within a year of the Edinburgh Conference, Ernst Troeltsch published *The Social Teaching of the Christian Churches*, the most systematic and comprehensive treatment of the interaction of Christian thought and social analysis yet undertaken. Central to his analysis was the question of Christian attitudes toward work, property, social class, and wealth and poverty. One year later, Troeltsch was invited to deliver some lectures. He spoke to the mood of the era; *Protestantism and Progress* was the result.

In this country, similar concerns prompted Walter Rauschenbusch to publish *For God and the People: Prayers for the Social Awakening*, one of the most widely read books of prayers of the century. It was followed by *Christianizing the Social Order*, with its earnest, populist proposal for "the democratization of economic life."

These developments set the agenda for twentieth-century Protestant reflections on economic issues and established the moral terms of debate for modern Protestant ecumenical witness. The priority of economic issues in this agenda has been deflected again and again by political threats to democracy—from the totalitarian left of Stalin and the totalitarian right of Hitler, and all their petty imitators. That gave rise to the "Christian Realism" that we properly associate with Reinhold Niebuhr. But on economic issues, he substantively shared the views that the ecumenical Protestant churches began to develop. The democratization of the economic order was the predominant theme of official statements, of scholarly work, and of attempts to reform popular piety.

That populist impetus has taken on a new spirit in today's world under the impact of Liberation Theology; we have seen a new positive assessment of what Marx might contribute to theology and ethics and a new ethical demand for a preferential option for the poor. Since 1966 internationally, and since 1976 in the United States specifically, ecumenically oriented Protestantism has been

---

sponsible World Society (Philadelphia: Westminster Press, 1974); and R. Preston, *Church and Society in the Late Twentieth Century* (London: SCM Press, 1982).

3. I discuss this point more fully in *Public Theology and Political Economy*, especially chapter 4.

caught up in a significant debate about what this new spirit means.[4] One interesting feature of this debate is the attacks that Protes- tantism has experienced from within itself—notably, charges that it is holding to presuppositions that lead it to alliances with the forces of oppression.[5] It is as yet unclear how much the debate will be shaped by the deeper roots of Protestantism or how it will be re- solved. But it is clear that the new debate challenges root assump- tions of Protestantism.

THE REFORMATION ROOTS

It may well serve our understanding of the prospects for Protes- tantism to consider some of the core presuppositions of its back- ground. Religious movements, like civilizations, have a certain inner charter. A constituting vision of a metaphysical-moral sort is the cornerstone of every profound religion.[6] That vision can un- dergo considerable modification. It can develop to explicit expres- sion what was only implicit earlier. It can recognize that the pre- sumptions underlying its overt message need clarification. It can combine or recombine with various social, political, scientific, or economic philosophies, interests, and institutions. And it can mod- ify its accents in the face of new conditions—subordinating some matters that were thought to be weighty previously and raising pre- viously secondary themes to matters of primary importance.[7]

But, despite all this, a religious movement cannot deny the core

---

4. With regard to the international context, see *Economic Growth in World Perspective*, ed. Denis Munby (New York: Association Press, 1966); and *Responsible Government in a Revolutionary Age*, ed. Z. K. Mathews (New York: Association Press, 1966). On the specifically American con- text, see Sergio Torres and John Eagleson, *Theology in the Americas* (Mary- knoll, N.Y.: Orbis Books, 1976).

5. For examples of such charges, see Rubem Alves, *Protestantism and Repression: A Brazilian Case Study*, trans. John Drury (Maryknoll, N.Y.: Orbis Books, 1985); and Beverly W. Harrison, *Making the Connections: Es- says in Feminist Social Ethics*, ed. Carol S. Robb (Boston: Beacon Press, 1985).

6. Troeltsch was surely correct when he wrote that "Protestantism is . . . in the first place a religious force, and only in the second or third sense a civilizing force. . . . To understand this we only need to grasp the elementary truths, that religious forces really only proceed from religious motives" (*Protestantism and Progress*, trans. W. Montgomery [Boston: Bea- con Press, 1958], p. 175).

7. This concept is implicit in the work of Weber and Troeltsch; I have developed it by tracing key interactions of piety, polity, and policy in an article entitled "Politics and Religion" in the *Encyclopedia of Religion*, ed. Mircea Eliade (New York: Macmillan, 1986).

vision that gave it birth and still claim to be what it was. Such a denial renders it something other than it was. For centuries, Catholics accused Protestants of breaking not only with the church but with Christianity. Today, some Protestants wonder whether the new Liberation Theology accents that demand, above all, a theological accountability to the poor have done the same. And that, of course, is part of the question before us: Has modern ecumenically oriented Protestantism become something other than catholic and Protestant Christianity? And if it has not, should it in the future? Are we, or ought we to be, as Paul Tillich put the question in 1927, at "the end of the Protestant era"?[8]

The original Reformers would not, of course, have understood our questions. They would all immediately have pointed out that we are accountable to God and God alone. We have a Savior in Jesus Christ; no other person or group can save humanity. And while we are, within limits, to be obedient to properly appointed rulers, it is precisely the message of the Reformation that we are, in an ultimate sense, accountable to no class of humans, whether rich or poor, whether parent or prince or priest or pauper. We are, of course, to care for the neighbor in need, but the point of all the upheaval is precisely that our accountability to God must take priority over all other loyalties. Nor would the Reformers quite have understood our sense of the development of new, constructive perspectives out of old traditions by the intentional rearrangement of them for sociopolitical purposes, as the Social Gospel at the turn of the century and Liberation Theology currently proposes. That, they would have argued, is precisely what the Roman Church had been doing for centuries—losing, in the process, the core vision of the early church and the Scriptures. The very notion that humans can and should do such things is what has led to the new "Babylonian captivity," the "Aristotelian church," and the "betrayal of Christ," as Luther so picturesquely puts it. What is needed above all, said the Reformers, is the recovery of that which had been obscured by all such human accretions—the fact that we are justified by grace through faith alone.

That is not to say that the Reformation did not reconstruct or had nothing to say about our responsibilities to the poor. Luther, Calvin, and Müntzer—the three most important leaders of the Protestant Reformation in the sixteenth century with respect to our question—were all convinced that the reappropriation of the gospel and a renewed sense of accountability to God would issue in new concern

---

8. See Tillich, *The Protestant Era* (Chicago: University of Chicago, 1948); see also *The Thought of Paul Tillich*, ed. James L. Adams et al. (San Francisco: Harper & Row, 1985), especially chapters 1, 2, and 16.

for the neighbor in need. But each of these Reformers places an emphasis on a different aspect of trinitarian faith, an emphasis that shapes his response to poverty.

Luther

The core of Luther's protest was not economic but spiritual. It was, however, connected to material life in a number of ways—not least by the economic practices of his day. The medieval church, like every institution, required financing, and practices such as the sale of indulgences were the surface manifestation of a number of attempts to preserve an elaborate edifice of priestly organization to mediate sacerdotal grace to temporal humanity. It was assumed that the spiritual estates had special access to divine grace and that it was their vocation to mediate that grace to the people. The temporal estates, in turn, had access to material resources, and it was their vocation to offer them up to God by giving them to the church. This grand trade-off had given shape to Christendom for several centuries.

But behind this distinction between the spiritual and temporal estates was the fundamental assumption of what Lovejoy called the "great chain of being," which implied what Troeltsch called the "cosmos of callings,"[9] what was assumed to be manifest in a fixed hierarchy of persons. Still deeper, this metaphysical-moral vision rested on a fundamental distinction between soul and body. Just as the soul was understood to be superior to the body, so the spiritual was considered superior to the carnal, the clergy superior to the laity, the *sacerdotum* superior to the *imperium*, and the life of *orare* superior to the life of *labore*.

Moved by deep personal and spiritual anguish, Luther challenged these presuppositions—at least some of them—on the basis of his personal discovery of Pauline Christology. He concluded that the decisive struggle between the spiritual and the carnal should not be institutionalized in a hierarchy of persons. Sanford Lakoff grasped this point when he wrote that for Luther

> the conflict between soul and body was a problem *for all Christians* in *every calling* they pursued. When Paul told the Galatians, "Walk in the Spirit and you shall not fulfill the lust of the flesh," he gave this counsel "not only unto hermits and monks, . . . but unto all Christians." Nor is the meaning of "fleshly lust" confined to sexuality . . . , for it applies just as much to "spir-

---

9. See especially chapters 2 and 3 of Troeltsch's *Social Teaching of the Christian Churches*, trans. Olive Wyon (New York: Harper, 1932).

itual" temptations. . . . Hence the Papists "are madmen, not understanding what the spirit is or what the flesh is."[10]

The implications of such a criticism are vast. It spurred publication of the Bible in the vernacular so that ordinary people could see for themselves what the text says. It implied new definitions of baptism and communion and a new sense of brotherhood and sisterhood in the church—in contrast to the fatherhood of the priests and childhood of laity. It gave rise to the celebrated notion of "the priesthood of all believers." Luther established, in theological principle, something that became a common accent in all of Protestantism—the spiritual equality of all believers. Indeed, "to suggest that the spiritual equality of Christians was at all applicable to social institutions, even if only to the church, was to question seriously not only the distinction between earthly servitude and ideal equality, upon which both ecclesiastical and secular hierarchy had found firm support, but also the later medieval attempt to justify both ecclesiastical and civil hierarchy by analogy with the hierarchy of the heavens."[11]

But Luther did not fully and consistently carry out the implications of his evangelical insight for other institutional areas. When the peasants thought they had found in his doctrines the warrants for economic and political revolution, he called on the established powers to crush them.[12] Perhaps the fact that he depended on the German princes to defend him against Roman troops also played a role in his high regard for obedience to political authority. More profoundly, his sharp distinction between law and gospel, understood as outer and inner, led him to accept a *Realpolitik* that dominated the exterior structures of life and short-circuited the renewal of societal forms. In any event, these are the charges that other branches of the Reformation have laid on Luther and his legacy.

For whatever reason, it does seem clear that Luther's views comport with one of Troeltsch's theses—that Christianity does not contain within itself the resources to construct a Christian social philosophy entirely out of the gospel. Wherever a social ethic develops in Christianity, it always involves an alliance of doctrine with social theories and political philosophies beyond the doctrine itself. Particular views of the core nature of the gospel lead believers to adopt particular social theories, but a theologically based social ethic develops only when a biblically rooted faith incorporates philoso-

---

10. Lakoff, *Equality in Political Philosophy* (Boston: Beacon Press, 1967), p. 28.

11. Lakoff, *Equality in Political Philosophy,* p. 30.

12. See Luther, "An Open Letter to the Christian Nobility," in *Three Treatises* (Philadelphia: Muhlenberg Press, 1943).

phies and social theories of some civilization. The kind and quality of "secular" thought with which faith joins profoundly affects the way a Christian social ethic is developed. And in this respect Luther was essentially an unreconstructed medieval thinker.

Platonism, as mediated through the neo-Platonists (it is not incidental that Luther was an Augustinian monk before his break with Rome), held that some people are born to special roles in the community and that these are essentially unalterable. Luther continued to assume this sort of hierarchical "cosmos of vocations" in the world even though he had challenged it in the community of faith. It is important to note that Luther was, in a sense, more a Protestant than a Reformer: he was at his best routing out basic Christological insights he believed had been betrayed by false alliance with artificial human constructions. He could "negate the negations" of the gospel with wondrous vitriol. But "reforming" entails having a clear sense of the form upon which the common life ought to be restructured, and Luther never quite had that. It was his vision that we ought all to infuse the station in life in which we find ourselves with a new spirit, a new love, a new charity, a new diligence, a new dignity. We ought all to be what we are truly born to be, but with a new disposition. The old forms of civilizational order thus remain basically intact.

This is not to say that Luther's views had no implications for the overcoming of poverty. He was quite concerned about poverty and its effects, and this concern moves in several directions of considerable importance to subsequent Christianity and history. For one thing, he gave work a new dignity. He overturned the view that physical labor was subordinate in value to spiritual labor: slopping the hogs, brewing the beer, and changing the baby's diaper are quite as spiritual as the work of cardinals and abbots, he once wrote to his beloved Kate. He transformed the ascetic injunction of the monastic, *orare et labore*, to a new asceticism in the heart of each worker: *labore est orare*, if done in the right spirit. And this can lead to new wealth. Lakoff points out that it was Luther, and not some latter-day laissez-faire economist, who wrote that if someone

> wishes to be rich, let him put his hand to the plow and seek his riches in the earth! It is enough if the poor are decently cared for, so that they do not die of hunger or of cold. It is not fitting that one man should live in idleness on another's labor, or be rich and live comfortably at the cost of another's discomfort, according to the present perverted custom.[13]

---

13. From "Trade and Usury," in *Luther's Works*, vol. 45, ed. Walther I. Brandt (Philadelphia: Muhlenberg Press, 1962), pp. 233-310.

Yet Luther was by no means an advocate of free trade in any sense. He shared with the medieval period a deep suspicion of trade, commerce, and finance of all kinds and thought that they should be politically regulated.[14] His peasant experience (not a little influenced by both German nationalism and anti-Semitism) supported with the rather elaborate body of medieval teaching that only the earth was fecund, and that manufacture and exchange, investment and interest, corporations and banks—indeed any economic gains made outside the direct control of family and government—were nothing more than sophisticated forms of stealing by artifice. Allowing such practices simply gave license to greed. They made Germans poor by taking the raw products of agrarian communities to foreign lands in exchange for luxury items that only the elite could afford. "Foreign trade," he wrote, which

> brings from Calcutta and India and such places wares like costly silks, articles of gold, and spices—which minister only to ostentation but serve no useful purpose, and which drain away the money from land and people—would not be permitted if we had [proper] government and princes. . . . England would have less gold if Germany let her keep her cloth; the king of Portugal would have less if we let him keep his spices. Count up how much cash is taken out of Germany, without need of reason, . . . and you will wonder how it happens that there is still a heller [a half-pfennig] left in German lands.[15]

At the local as well as the national level, Luther was deeply concerned with the problem of poverty. Like all the early Reformers, he viewed it as having a double nature. On the one hand, begging had been institutionalized as an acceptable practice for priests, monks, and nuns for several centuries.[16] Luther had little patience for voluntary or "evangelical" poverty of this sort; he believed that it resulted from a misunderstanding of the gospel and that those who practiced it were leeches on others. "No monk . . . or church beggar shall be permitted or allowed to beg or have others beg for him in our parish, . . . city or . . . villages," he stated; indeed, "*anyone* not incapacitated by reason of age or illness shall work or, with the aid of

---

14. See John T. Noonan, Jr., *The Scholastic Analysis of Usury* (Cambridge: Harvard University Press, 1967).

15. Luther, "Trade and Usury," pp. 246-47.

16. On this point, I am grateful to E. McKee for drawing my attention to T. Fischer's *Staedtische Armut und Armenfuersorge in 15. und 16. Yahrhundert* (Otto Schwartz, 1979); and B. Tierney's *Medieval Poor Law* (Berkeley and Los Angeles: University of California Press, 1959).

the authorities, be expelled from the parish, the city, and the villages."[17]

On the other hand, as a pastor Luther recognized that some individuals were impoverished by age, illness, or other circumstances, and that these needed the support of others. To this end, he advocated the founding and careful administration of a common chest by trustees elected from the parish, locked with four keys— one held by a representative of the nobility, one by a member of the council, one by a town citizen, and one by a rural peasant. The resources of this chest were to be collected from the "secularization" of ecclesiastical prebends and the contributions of nobles, citizens, artisans, and peasants.

In such teachings, we see evidence of attitudes toward poverty that have been a part of some branches of Protestantism ever since: a demand for and honoring of hard work and a contempt for any who claim spiritual superiority by avoiding productive labor; a personal regard for immediate neighbors as opposed to impersonal systems that link us to distant neighbors; a passive acceptance of the exterior structures by which the common life is organized, moderated by the infusion of such structures with an inner spirit of love that protects the less fortunate; and the formation of charitable institutions based in the church that treat all classes equitably.

Calvin

If Luther is the model "protester" of Protestantism, Calvin is the premier "reformer" of the Reformation. Calvin took much of what he believed directly from Luther, but a fundamentally different understanding of the relationship of law and gospel modified all his social views, and he read his Bible less through the lenses of the neo-Platonic hierarchies of medieval thought than through the cosmopolitan, Stoic-influenced jurisprudence he studied as a young lawyer. Nor was he captivated by the notion of equality that Luther had derived from his confidence in the spiritual capacity of every believer to heed the Word in the inwardness of the heart. Calvin was committed to equality, but it was an equality based also on a radical sense of the objectivity of sin and a saving God: all are equally sinners and all equally in need of salvation. He was indebted to Augustine less for hierarchical theories of community

---

17. Luther, "Ordinance of a Common Chest," in *Luther's Works,* 45:186.

than for a radical sense of a grace that constructs the City of God in the midst of the corrupt cities of the world.

The principle that we are justified by grace through faith implies a need for transformed patterns of thought and life. First of all, it demands an obedient regard for the justice and truth of the one true God, but the social corollary of this view is that the "natural" structures of the common life are rooted in corruption, and so they have to be reordered according to godly principles. It is on such theocentric bases that Calvin develops a "public theology" that has, as André Biéler says, "inspired his followers with the most uncompromising social conservatism as well as with the boldest revolutionary socialism."[18]

Like Luther, Calvin remained a medieval man in many ways. He shared the "Constantinian" presupposition that the church is to be established and protected by political power. He did not depart from the predominant practices of the day when heretics, such as Servetus, threatened to disrupt common belief by teaching unorthodox views of the Trinity, for example. And while he was eager to displace the rule of popes and bishops in temporal life, his notion of the elect was liable to distortion into new forms of theocratic domination. Tolerance was not his strong point.

Yet Calvin also accented several motifs that shaped the subsequent development of some Protestant attitudes toward poverty. Most striking among these motifs are his God-centered understandings of "vocation" and "covenant," which significantly modify the medieval Catholic and Lutheran notions of the "cosmos of vocations." I have already noted elsewhere that,

> As Max Weber argued in his seminal treatment of the Protestant ethic, both Lutherans and Calvinists perceive the secular calling as a decisive arena in which to work out one's God-given duty.... Calvinists, however, do not necessarily affirm that the structure of social roles is pregiven by God in creation. God's will is dynamic, and new roles may be required as God works out his purposes through recalcitrant humanity. And, while humans are viewed as essentially sinners, the power and grace of God is such that *we can become what we are not*. The Calvinists affirm the possibility of *transformation*—not only of the inner heart but of the outer organization of life.... Beyond justification there is the obligation, bestowed on us in God's call to duty, to "sanctify," to make holy and righteous, both the person *and*

---

18. Biéler, *The Social Humanism of Calvin*, trans. Paul T. Fuhrmann (Richmond: John Knox Press, 1964), p. 27.

the social world in which persons live. To carry out this "sancti-fication," people may rearrange social roles; they may "reform" social, economic, and political institutions in accord with God's law, purpose, and love. . . . Thus, the Calvinists affirmed the . . . right to change things, to do things in a new way.[19]

And change things they did. There may be squabbles among scholars as to how much of the transition to modern structures of law, politics, and family life was induced by Calvin and the Calvin-ists compared to other influences, but few dispute that it was sub-stantial.[20] Social life was suddenly rendered less fixed in order, more malleable to transformation, at least for those who began to grasp the transcendent levers by which to move the world. By appeal to "vocation," peasants and artisans could be called to become entre-preneurs and magistrates; by appeal to "covenant," traditional com-munal bonds could be broken and new societal patterns con-structed. And since both are rooted in the providential will of God—which entails both a structured order and a dynamic free-dom—the task for humans is to reconstruct life by a disciplined, ra-tional exercise of the will under godly standards.

These motifs are directly connected to the radical notion that nothing we do can assure our salvation. God's providential will alone settles that issue. And while some who followed this reason-ing arrived at a kind of spiritual fatalism, most found relief in it. Our ultimate salvation is God's responsibility, not ours. Not even "faith-ing" harder can change that. Calvinists felt themselves liberated from religious preoccupations to attend religiously to their occupa-tions—discerned and lived out as "vocations" in the reform of eccle-siastical, civil, social, and economic life in this world according to the principles of "covenant." Similarly, they felt liberated from their "communities" of origin and called to construct "societies" on new foundations.[21] The implications of this message led, on the one hand,

---

19. *Creeds, Society, and Human Rights*, p. 59.

20. On the Calvinist impact on law, see David E. Little, *Religion, Order, and Law: A Study in Pre-Revolutionary England* (New York: Harper, 1969); and Harold J. Berman, *Law and Revolution: The Formation of the Western Legal Tradition* (Cambridge: Harvard University Press, 1983). On politics, see Sheldon S. Wolin, *Politics and Vision: Continuity and Innovation in Western Political Thought* (Boston: Little, Brown, 1960); and Michael Walzer, *The Revolution of the Saints* (New York: Atheneum, 1968). On family life, see James T. Johnson, *A Society Ordered by God* (Nashville: Abingdon, 1970); and Edmund Leites, *The Puritan Conscience and Modern Sexuality* (New Haven: Yale University Press, 1986).

21. The important differences between communal and societal un-derstandings of the common life are classically stated by Ferdinand Ton-

to a new courage for personal rights and, on the other, to a new "associationalism."[22]

Any who wish to understand the long-range effect of such thinking will have to continue to wrestle with the vast body of literature deriving from the arguments of Weber and Troeltsch.[23] Sadly, Weber and Troeltsch are widely misunderstood on both the right and the left wings of contemporary social and historical research because nearly all current analysts misconstrue the meaning of the term *capitalism* in their work. They did not, as is now widely assumed, use the term in contrast to socialism; in fact, they are basically concerned with the core contrast of modern, rationalized, social economies, whether capitalist or socialist (Weber calls the latter "state-capitalist"), with traditional, communitarian, and household-based economies. Current misunderstandings of the Weberian arguments on this point are both a testimony to the triumph of Marxist distinctions in common discourse and evidence of a certain sociological sloppiness on the part of a number of intellectual historians.[24]

It is true, however, that neither Weber nor his disciples base their arguments on close examination of Calvin's teachings and practices with respect to wealth and poverty. While much work remains to be done in this area, my colleague Elsie McKee has made more careful progress than most. In her study "Social Welfare Reform in the Sixteenth Century," she points out that the reformers faced a series of

> social problems for which old solutions no longer worked. By most accounts, medieval ecclesiastical charity managed adequately until about the fourteenth century. . . . [But] with the coming of the bubonic plague, the hundred years war, and the increasing challenges to ecclesiastical and feudal authorities, old securities broke down. Hordes of wandering peasants and soldiers posed a vagrancy problem of unheard of propor-

---

nies in *Community and Society,* ed. Charles P. Loomis (New York: Harper, 1957).

22. On this, see *Voluntary Associations: A Study of Groups in Free Societies,* ed. D. B. Robertson (Richmond: John Knox Press, 1966); and *Voluntary Associations,* Nomes Series, vol. 11, ed. J. Roland Pennock and John W. Chapman (New York: Atherton Press, 1969).

23. A good place to start would be *The Protestant Ethic and Modernization: A Comparative View,* ed. Schmuel N. Eisenstadt (New York: Basic Books, 1968).

24. As has been demonstrated by R. Gill in an unpublished paper entitled "Historians' Misinterpretations of Weber" (1981), the misunderstanding is largely due to the influence of R. H. Tawney's *Religion and the Rise of Capitalism* (New York: Harcourt, Brace, 1926).

tions. . . . The cities were faced with the greatest problems and therefore became the pioneers in social welfare reform.[25]

Calvin was among those who introduced new teachings and practices in this area. New restrictions on begging had already been introduced, although absolute prohibition was new to both Lutheran and Calvinist locales; the centralization and laicization of control over charity funds is evidently part of the story, but that had also been advocated by the humanists; and the change from voluntary to compulsory support of poor relief programs seems significant, but some Catholics also attempted this. McKee argues that all of these together were "rationalized" into new patterns of administration. That, perhaps compounded by "the emphasis on work," shifted the whole pattern of response to poverty.

As McKee points out, Calvin "desacralized poverty" more radically than perhaps any of the other Reformers; and he "resacralized" concern for organized benevolence and welfare by making diaconal service to the poor a central office for laity in the church and the city.[26] But it was not only care for the poor that he "resacralized," it was also care for those who labor.

> God assigns an earthly goal to his creature. Man is created to work. . . . "The blessing of the Lord," says Calvin, "is on the hands of him who works. Certainly God curses laziness and loafing." . . . Since work is this indispensable operation by which man becomes accomplished in his obedience to God and without which man is neither a man nor a Christian, unemployment is a social scourge which must be fought and denounced with extreme vigor. For to deprive man of his work is truly a crime. . . . It is equivalent to taking away his life. . . . "Concerning artisans and workingmen, . . . to deprive them of this necessary means is equivalent to cutting their throats."[27]

But Calvin also sanctifies work in precisely those areas where Luther (and the Catholic traditions) found severe moral temptation. Commerce, trade, manufacture, and banking are proper arenas of sanctified labor in Calvin's eyes; indeed, they are essential to the common life, for material exchange shows the interdependence of individuals in society and of societies in the international context. In

---

25. McKee, *John Calvin on the Diaconate and Liturgical Almsgiving* (Geneva: Librairie Droz, 1984), pp. 93-94. McKee unintentionally confirms the Weber hypothesis in this work.
26. See McKee, *John Calvin on the Diaconate and Liturgical Almsgiving*, pp. 124ff.
27. Biéler, *The Social Humanism of Calvin*, p. 45.

a move widely recognized as revolutionary, Calvin rejected the conviction that money (the symbol of complex, nonagrarian economies) is not fecund and that all proper production is related to the fecundity of land. He understood the nature of money and usury in a new way. He remained aware of the danger of worshiping Mammon, of course, but he asserted that the circulation of money through commerce, investments, and working capital can also be redemptive. It can bind together in common interests people not previously connected, it can produce more wealth for the relief of need and for the benefit of all, and it can free us from pagan loyalties to a "tribal brotherhood" and give us a new appreciation of "universal otherhood," as Benjamin Nelson puts it in his remarkable study of this shift.[28]

Calvin moved beyond an ethic of and for distribution to develop an ethic of and for production. The goal of commerce, trade, and investment is holy in his view. Although these arenas are fraught with moral and spiritual peril, believers ought not to shrink from the temptations but steel their souls to engage them, he says. The whole purpose of production

> is to procure for each man whatever he needs in order to live. Commerce must relieve the pain of man and render his existence pleasant. . . . When turned away from its divine purposes, commerce rapidly changes its nature. [Then] fraud and dishonesty make economic relationships practically impossible. . . . Dishonesty in business, therefore, is not only a fault against human morality; it is a sacrilege.[29]

Further, Calvin maintains that the quest for reasonable gain from commerce, trade, and investment—profit—ought not to be motivated by greed. Indeed, he identifies the very success of such industry with the rational restraint of greed. He recognized avarice, hording, and the ostentatious display of wealth as perennial temptations. But he distinguished reasonable profit from these. Jesus Christ had himself approved of return on wise and prudential investment in the parable of the talents, said Calvin. What is gained fairly in diligent stewardship under the mandate of the righteous God is to be honored. It should be invested quickly that it might not be horded and that the unemployed might be given work, to the benefit of the whole human community. And it should be super-

---

28. Nelson, *The Idea of Usury: From Tribal Brotherhood to Universal Otherhood*, 2d ed. (Chicago: University of Chicago Press, 1969).
29. Biéler, *The Social Humanism of Calvin*, p. 51.

vised by both church and state authorities, who are appointed agents of the sovereign God, so that the radical sinfulness of humanity will not destroy the fragile bonds of mutuality and trust that business both requires and so easily subverts in the human commonwealth.

In light of these motifs, it is not difficult to see why Calvinism both changed the world and opened new possibilities that have variously combined—in ages less certain of the laws and purposes of God, when vocation is transformed into division of labor and covenant becomes but a pragmatic contract—with individualistic market theories of economics and with the collectivistic, planned economies of modern socialisms. Both of these combinations falsify Calvin's legacy, however, for they ignore (as Weber also did) the ecclesiological dimensions of Calvin's thought.[30] That demanded a church discipline over character and behavior as well as a strong but limited state.[31]

Müntzer

The third "sectarian" stream of Protestantism has frequently been the wild card in Protestant thought about economic issues. If Catholicism tried to penetrate and shape civilization from above, and if Luther tried to infuse it with a new spirit of Christ from within, and if Calvin attempted to reform it with engaged action in the midst of life on the basis of godly standards that transcend life, this third stream is marked by its suspicion of civilization. It holds the "world" to be faithless and decadent, beyond redemption or reform except through a radical, eschatological transformation: nothing less than a total conversion by the dynamic power of the Holy Spirit can save humanity.

A plethora of movements were engendered by convictions like these and facilitated by the loosening bonds of control at the hands of the church—although this is certainly relative: Catholic, Lutheran, and Calvinist leaders alike persecuted these religious "subversives." Some, as Troeltsch pointed out long ago, tended to be "withdrawing," while others were "aggressive."

The subversives did not think that human beings could bring about the necessary transformation in civilization at large. They

---

30. See James L. Adams, "The Protestant Ethic with Fewer Tears," in *On Being Human Religiously* (Boston: Beacon Press, 1986).

31. For more on this, see my *Creeds, Society, and Human Rights*, especially chapters 3 and 4.

tended to form sectarian groups who wanted little more than sufficient peace to try to live out their spiritual and ethical visions of the
gospel in their little conventicles "until he come." They formed net-
works of self-governed "base communities" of worship and work,
trying to live according to the Spirit in the interstices of society—
when they were not on the run from magisterial Christians. They
tried to reenact in their own lives and in the protodemocracies of
their communities of faith the patterns and principles of primitive
Christianity, not unsatisfied to be at the margins of civilization.

The aggressive sectarians felt that the judgment of God was
about to bring history to an end by force, and they considered themselves agents of the chiliastic vengeance against civilization and its
pretenses, its exploitations, its corruptions.

But between these extremes were many variations that simply
do not fit Troeltsch's distinction, as George H. Williams has so ad-
mirably documented.[32] And Thomas Müntzer is among these.
Above all, Müntzer understood Christianity essentially as "movement," inspired above all by the movement of the Holy Spirit in history. He introduced to Protestantism a new conception of how God
and spirituality relate to human material history—a conception already in some measure familiar to Catholicism because of the influence of Joachim of Fiora and the "spiritual Franciscans."[33] God was
bringing new possibilities into the midst of history as we ap-
proached a "new age of the Spirit," said Müntzer, and Christians
should move with the Spirit wherever it was shattering old forms
and bringing new hopes.

There is quite another reason for taking Müntzer as the symbol
of this "third stream." In the nineteenth century, Frederick Engels
treated Müntzer as a primary forerunner of the coming Communist
revolution in his influential tract *The Peasant War in Germany*. Subsequent scholarship has shown this interpretation to be less than
adequate; Müntzer was both more theological and less communist

---

32. See Williams, *The Radical Reformation* (Philadelphia: Westminster
Press, 1962); and his introduction to *Spiritual and Anabaptist Writers*
(Philadelphia: Westminster, 1957).

33. I think Lakoff is quite correct in suggesting this in his *Equality in
Political Philosophy*, pp. 48-59.

34. See Bloch's *Thomas Müntzer als Theologe der Revolution* (Berlin:
Aufbau Verlag, 1962), which is, by my reading, a summary and an exposi-
tion of the historical roots of his *Das Prinzip Hoffnung* (Frankfurt am Main:
Suhrkamp, 1959), which was so influential on many contemporary theo-
logians. On this, see *New Theology*, no. 5, ed. Martin E. Marty and D. G.
Peerman (New York: Macmillan, 1967).

than Engels wanted him to be. But in our own century, the socialist revisionist Ernst Bloch has more carefully shown ways in which Müntzer and Marx do in fact share radical human hopes for salvation through historical change—if and when Marxism does not become a bureaucratized, secularized, established "theocracy" of antitheistic ideology.[34] And, in recent decades, Bloch's ideas have become influential among those advocates of Liberation Theology who have searched for its roots.[35] Such observations suggest that many of the most important features of Liberation Theology, as they reflect an understanding of Christian accountability to the poor, derive not from specific "Third-World" contexts, as advertised, but from a deeply rooted "third stream" of Christian pneumatology— and they are now being applied to new contexts with but slender connection to Christological and theological accents.

Müntzer agreed with other Protestants in their criticisms of both the Roman Catholic Church and the humanists, but he disagreed with the "magisterial" Protestants about their sense of the authority of Scripture and reason and their solicitous concern to preserve civilization by reformation. Müntzer stressed the more direct experience of the Holy Spirit, to be grasped most immediately in the experience of suffering, as Christ did in the Passion and as simple people do in daily life. The Spirit turns all who experience it into prophets. Luther's "priesthood of all believers" quickly became a new "prophethood of all believers," most evident among those who are poor, miserable, and marginalized. And what Calvin later spoke of in terms of "vocation" and "covenant" was treated by Müntzer in terms of the spiritually possessed/materially dispossessed joining in a movement as "fighters and heralds" of what God was bringing about in history—"a revolution from below to be undertaken by an armed community of prophets."[36] "The whole world," Müntzer wrote, "must become prophetic in order that it may discern the true prophets."[37] And if it will not, the godless will be exterminated. If "violence should be done by us, the world and especially the pious

35. For examples, see Matthew L. Lamb, *Solidarity with Victims: Toward a Theology of Social Transformation* (New York: Crossroad, 1982); and, from a very different point of view, Dale Vree, *On Synthesizing Marxism and Christianity* (New York: Wiley-Interscience, 1967).

36. Lakoff, *Equality in Political Philosophy*, p. 54. And see N. Cohn, *The Pursuit of the Millennium* (New York: Harper, 1961).

37. Müntzer, "A Highly Provoked Defense and Answer to the Unspiritual, Soft-Living Flesh in Wittenberg," in *Leben und Scriften*, ed. O. H. Brandt (Jena, 1933), p. 525.

elect will know why we suffer and that we become identical with Jesus Christ."[38]

Müntzer and his movement were crushed by blood and iron, but his basic understanding of what the gospel is all about did not die. It went underground. It furtively combined with subsequent elements of Lutheran, Calvinist, and, indeed, some branches of Catholic thought. But, as we shall see, it was destined to return in new forms in modern, secular philosophies of history—and it is through these back channels that it has again become a force in the present.

BETWEEN THEN AND NOW

It is neither possible nor necessary to trace all the pertinent developments that transformed sixteenth-century Protestantism into modern ecumenical Protestantism. We have already reviewed the essential elements of the constituting visions. But since they did not remain in their pristine forms over time, it may be useful to trace, briefly, four recombinations of these elements that have helped define the contours of modern ecumenical Protestantism.

Pietism

Frequently pilloried by those who are interested in questions of economic justice and poverty, Pietism developed in the seventeenth century out of the interaction of forces expressed most powerfully in the sixteenth. The sectarian impulse, deeply influenced by an emphasis on the spiritual blessedness of the poor as we have here encountered it in Müntzer, was reconstituted in a less militant form that accented the blessedness of the poor in spirit. Over time, this impulse was integrated into Lutheranism and "evangelicalism" of many stripes. Wherever it spread, it engendered the formation of new communities of intense personal responsibility and a profound commitment to charitable care of the poor. Diaconal service to the dispossessed through hospitals for the sick, schools for the simple, soup for the hungry, and homes for widows and orphans has been understood as a major mark of the presence of the Spirit. Pietism's comparative neglect of or even repudiation of intentional social transformation has made it subject to sharp criticism by modern

---

38. Müntzer, "Sermon before Princes," in *Spiritual and Anabaptist Writers.*

heirs of Calvin and Müntzer,[39] although there is now no country in
the world where these efforts are not honored and needed. Indeed,
it can be argued that when the inner personal conviction to care for
the poor as a mark of true piety is not cultivated, the social will to
provide such care evaporates among the people, and governments
are unlikely to take on the task either. What social services are provided are often given grudgingly, coldly, and simply as a matter of
state interest.

Puritanism

So fateful for economic life in Anglo-American history, and therefore for enormous segments of the world economy today, Puritanism arose as a result of the the interaction of Calvinist and sectarian Protestantism. It is well documented that in Cromwell's
revolution, a century after Luther and Calvin, it took primarily a
political rather than an economic direction and in doing so was decisive in the formation of modern democratic institutions, in the establishment of human rights in civil and political areas, and in the
social and cultural establishment of the Protestant work ethic.[40] To
be sure, the diggers and levelers of the period echoed Müntzer on
some economic questions, but like him they were crushed.

It is less recognized that the covenantal theories of ecclesiology
advanced by the Puritans drew people into new, disciplined associations for production. The Puritans were suspicious of rampant individualism in religion, politics, and economics. Because some
branches of later Puritanism found themselves allied with laissez-
faire economics, it is seldom noted that these revisionist heirs of Calvin demanded that everyone be attached to a disciplined group.
Does Genesis not say "It is not good that man should be alone"?[41]

In a complicated history in which Puritan lawyers played a decisive role, this concern evolved into the consolidation of laws that
have shaped the modern limited-liability corporation. When the industrial revolution came to England, and subsequently to the
United States, the Puritan organizational form was present to exploit it. Furthermore, Puritan "economic associationalism," which
is neither individualistic nor collectivistic and neither familial nor

---

39. See Arend Th. van Leeuwen, *Prophecy in a Technocratic Age* (New
York: Scribner's, 1968).

40. On this, see my *Creeds, Society, and Human Rights*, especially
chapter 3.

41. See E. Digby Baltzell, *Puritan Boston and Quaker Philadelphia* (Boston: Beacon Press, 1982).

political, provided the institutional base for a distinct kind of
economic pluralism. Failure to grasp this point is one of the more
significant weaknesses of both capitalist and socialist economists'
efforts to understand the character of contemporary economic life.[42]

The many attempts to understand modern Western economic
systems on the basis of distinctions between "private" and "public"
or in terms of tensions between individual and political economic
interests simply ignore the primary social forms that shape modern
Western economies. This is true of those economists who, as heirs of
Adam Smith or Karl Marx, take it on faith that no good can come out
of Nazareth—or out of social analysis based in theology. It is also
true, however, of those Catholics who emphasize the twin values of
the human person and the common good as the poles of ethics, of
those Lutherans who accent the inner attitude of Christ in a received
cosmos of vocations, of those Christian socialists (often indirect
heirs of Müntzer) who see the corporations as no more than a mask
for greed and the preservation of private property, and of Third
World thinkers living in cultures where laws to govern corporate life
are not well developed and where the corporations are typically introduced by the traditional elite of the West to ensure efficient exploitation of the peasants.[43]

But regardless of their confessional background, North Atlantic
peoples (and increasingly Pacific peoples as well) who today live in,
through, and from the corporate organization of social life engendered by the Puritan heritage find that the critiques based on
these other perspectives simply do not square with reality as they
know it. For the most part, on this issue the Protestant laity tend to
do as the majority of American Catholics do with respect to birth
control: they quietly ignore what the church leadership says and
doubt that the leaders have the experience to know what they are
talking about.

---

42. For more on this, see my *Public Theology and Political Economy*,
especially chapter 7.

43. Several newer studies claim to assert the preferential option for
the poor and yet remain critical of the sort of conceptions of what best
serves the poor that are typically associated with Liberation Theology.
Among them are Robert Benne's *The Ethic of Democratic Capitalism: A
Moral Reassessment* (Philadelphia: Fortress Press, 1981); Nathan
Rosenberg and L. E. Birdzell, Jr.'s *How the West Grew Rich: The Economic
Transformation of the Industrial World* (New York: Basic Books, 1986); Mi-
chael Novak's *Will It Liberate?* (New York: Paulist Press, 1986); and
Peter L. Berger's *Capitalist Revolution: Fifty Propositions about Prosperity,
Equality, and Liberty* (New York: Basic Books, 1986).

The Methodist and Baptist Traditions

Of all the branches of Protestantism, the Methodist and Baptist are the two that expanded most rapidly in the eighteenth and nineteenth centuries. Each is an outgrowth of new evangelical accents derived from Reformation roots as expanded and recombined in Pietism and Puritanism. The Baptists trace some of their deeper roots to the Anabaptist withdrawing sects of the sixteenth century but are more directly related to the Independent and Separatist Puritans of the seventeenth. The Methodists grew from the evangelical wing of Anglo-Catholic thought as stimulated by strong elements of both Pietism and Puritanism. Neither branch has viewed systematic theological work or the nurturing of the structures of civilization as central to faith. On this point, Pietism is stronger in its influence.

These late heirs of the Reformation have, more dramatically than their precursors, developed a populist emphasis. Their experiential, nondoctrinal character has made them more appealing to the unlettered. They have had more success converting miners, workers, farmers, and the marginalized into communities of ascetic self-discipline and hard work for the sake of the gospel (and the abundant life) than have the Lutherans, Calvinists, and Puritans. The pietist streak in them has prompted them to form charitable institutions of many kinds and inspired a sense of stewardship that is the envy of many other churches. Secular authors may chide them for failing to mobilize the masses, over which Methodist and Baptist preachers have had great influence in other respects, to participation in the kinds of transformations brought by the French Revolution; but those authors have also recognized that it is precisely the nurturing of self-governing "classes" (a Methodist hallmark) and "autonomous congregations" (a Baptist hallmark) that gave to those on the underside of modern industrial societies the organizational skills to form labor unions, political caucuses, and advocacy organizations on behalf of the poor.[44] Indeed, it is from just such groups that many of the most vigorous proponents of the Social Gospel came in the early twentieth century, and it is in such circles that one frequently finds the most vociferous Protestant advocates of Liberation Theology today.

---

44. On this, see James L. Adams, *Voluntary Associations: Socio-Cultural Analyses and Theological Interpretation*, ed. J. Ronald Engel (Chicago: Exploration Press, 1986); and Sara M. Evans and Harry C. Boyte, *Free Spaces: The Sources of Democratic Changes in America* (San Francisco: Harper & Row, 1986).

Both the Methodist and Baptist communions in the United States were split by the Civil War and the modernist-fundamentalist disputes that sprung up soon thereafter. The connectional ecclesiology of the Methodists helped secure victory for those who fought against slavery and permitted quicker healing of rifts in that body. The organizational leadership of modern Methodism, if not its laity, has in large part overcome the political conservatism of John Wesley and most of its earlier heritage. Because doctrinal matters are of less pronounced importance in this tradition than in a number of others, Methodists have felt more free to join other heirs of Pietism and Puritanism at the forefront of those ecumenical denominations celebrating and honoring those who work for social change by advocacy on behalf of the poor and identification with the oppressed. Practical ethical engagement is the focus of their faith. Not infrequently they subscribe to the slogan of the ecumenical Life and Work Movement—"Doctrine divides; service unites."

The organizational decentralization of the Baptists has kept its leadership in closer touch with populist sentiment at local levels. The Southern Baptists have been more effective than Northern Baptists in amassing numbers, maintaining control of local churches, and holding the confidence of the masses. Their conservatism on theological as well as political and economic issues and their "frontier evangelical" style remains intact in many respects. Two exceptions, however, are noteworthy. A very high percentage of the American black population is Baptist, and it is from that quarter that something of the echo of Müntzer can sometimes be heard in Baptist circles. Further, the churches associated with the American Baptist Convention broke with the forms of evangelicalism that tended toward fundamentalism in the early decades of the twentieth century. The black and American Baptist traditions have thus become more closely aligned with the social witness of ecumenical Protestantism.

Over the last two centuries, Pietism, Puritanism, and the Methodist and Baptist traditions have all been greatly influenced by the Enlightenment, and by the Romantic movement in its wake. Liberal and radical motifs from the Enlightenment have pressed all of Protestantism in the West to accept, or at least to ally with, the secular ideals of democracy, science, and rationality as they appear in all modern thought. For most Protestants, such an alliance is not terribly difficult, for they find within their own theologies and ecclesiologies tendencies that press in the same directions. As Catholicism interacted with Aristotle, and the Reformers with Neo-Platonic and Stoic thought, modern Protestantism has interacted with the legacies of Locke and Kant, despite the fact that these figures doubted both the possibility of secure knowledge of a transcendent reality and the reliability of Scripture.

Further, most of these Protestant streams empathize with certain accents from the Romantic reaction to Enlightenment rationalism. The inner, personal experience of meaning is very important to most parts of Protestantism. It has a deep appreciation of the role of "experience" of the Spirit as a touchstone of authority in religion, and therefore in politics and economics. Few went so far as Müntzer (or the Quakers, who carried spiritual-sectarian ideas to America) in holding that experience of the Spirit is more important than Scripture and reason, but most reserved a high place for it. Still, it would be strange if modern heirs of Luther (few of whom claim to experience justification in a flash of insight) or the modern heirs of the Pietists and Puritans (now rather distantly removed from the Great Awakenings) or the Baptists and Methodists (still not far removed from modern Revivalism) did not think that experience of the Spirit made a substantial difference in every area of life.

I shall not, in this paper, deal with the enormous growth of neo-evangelical, Pentecostal, and fundamentalist Christianity. While these are often referred to as Protestant, it is only recently that they have been recognized as major world movements, growing much faster around the world than any of the family of traditions I have traced. They constitute a separate topic in their own right. While most of these movements have not passed through the challenges of the Enlightenment, they do have affinities with Romanticism that make ecumenical Protestantism appear strangely cool, analytical, and nearly humanistic to them.

I feel justified in avoiding an extended treatment of these movements here for three reasons. First, the doctrines of these churches engender among the dispossessed (to whom they most frequently appeal) a characteristic attitude toward the "work ethic" similar to that which we have already seen in their Reformation, Pietist, Puritan, Methodist, and Baptist precursors. Second, the most important teachings on attitudes toward the poor which these groups now represent do not differ substantively from the major Protestant themes outlined above. And third, these movements have experienced much of their growth in contexts where the Liberation movements are also strong, and they are in the same position as ecumenical Protestant groups in having to decide what they think about these "new" options.

Historicism

There are many forms of historicism. We can find it in process philosophy, in much of phenomenology, and in the epistemological schools of nihilistic thinking from Nietzsche to Derrida. But it was Hegel more than any other single figure who recovered and recast the legacy of Müntzer for Protestant historicism. He was the decisive bridge between the radical reformation and the post-Marxian revisionists such as Ernst Bloch. He held that the clue to meaning could be found in the fact that the Spirit interacts with materiality dialectically to bring about the historical transformation of everything. In Hegel the third stream of Protestantism returned with intellectual vigor propounding a "scientific" metaphysics of history. It had, as before, a tendency toward totalism—everything had to be rethought from a new perspective, everything had to be reconstructed with a new consciousness. Family life, ethics, history, society, politics, law, and economics were all to be interpreted and explained on the new grounds of the Spirit, and all who resisted the inexorable dynamic and refused to adjust to its demands would be crushed by it.[45]

Hegel was a philosopher, not a prophet or a politician, but he was not above the desire to have all of theology and the whole of the Prussian empire kiss the hem of his garment. For most of a century, a good bit of both did so. But two thinkers fateful for modern Protestantism did so only dialectically—Kierkegaard and Marx. Kierkegaard feared that the garment of Hegel's scientific metaphysics of history cloaked a soulless emptiness. He turned Hegel inside out and reinvigorated the intense personal pietism that had traditionally accompanied Protestant thought. His existential "decisionism," for which no warrants could be given, has been much celebrated in many Protestant circles under the rubric "crisis theology." Marx doubted that the imperial character of Hegel's system had clothes of any material substance. He turned Hegel upside down and argued that it is not the Spirit that brings change in historical and material life, but material and social transformation that alters the spirit.

Hegel had argued that the "master-slave relationship" was decisive in the history of the world but that it was now about to be fully

---

45. These themes are especially clear in Hegel's *Philosophy of History*, trans. E. S. Haldane (Oxford: Oxford University Press, 1892), and in the concluding chapter of his *Philosophy of Right*, trans. T. M. Knox (Oxford: Oxford University Press, 1942).

and finally overcome by the further actualization of the Spirit in modern consciousness and civilization. Marx found neither modern consciousness nor modern civilization so promising. He saw exploitation under the surfaces of modernity. To account for that, he borrowed the idea of the master-slave relationship and turned it into the dialectic of the bourgeoisie and the proletariat, assigning the proletariat the role of chief agent in transforming the world. The workers of the world are particularly qualified to bring about this messianic transformation, he argued, because they are the doers and makers of society. The severity of their imposed poverty was finally stripping them of all illusions about the nature of "spiritual salvation." They were beginning to recognize that religion, theology, and all Spirit-based philosophies of history were merely ideological tools in the hands of the masters being used to control the slaves of the world. The proletariat, said Marx, would become the new prophets of *real* life, would usher in the new history, construct a new civilization, and indeed produce a new human spirit, which was already appearing among the vanguard.[46]

Marx's ideas contributed to a dramatic "resacralization of poverty," to the view that all thought, religion, politics, and economics must be accountable to the poor, for of such is the new, quite material kingdom of heaven on earth. When the spirit of this earthly historicism is linked to an existential decisionism in the tradition of Kierkegaard, religious authenticity is determined by choosing the option for the poor.

Liberation Theology, which depends heavily on this historicist metaphysics, now poses intensely sharp questions to ecumenical Protestantism. Currently its energy comes more from the Catholic than the Protestant adaptations of these motifs. But it is notable that Catholics find in it new confrontations with modes of thought from the Enlightenment and from Romanticism, and since modern Protestantism has already adopted much from these movements, it is already conditioned to embrace this new refinement as simply another step along the way. Moreover, this historicism is beginning to influence the dynamic Pentecostal, evangelical, independent Baptist, pietist, and fundamentalist movements now gaining popularity among the dispossessed in Asia, Africa, and Latin America. Overall, the tendency is to embrace entirely or to repudiate utterly the vision of accountability to the poor it brings. Only a few evangelical

---

46. Such an interpretation of the connections of Hegel and Marx can be seen in Arend Th. van Leeuwen's *Critique of Heaven, Critique of Earth,* 2 vols. (New York: Scribner's, 1972).

leaders with deep sympathy for these movements seem able to be selective.[47]

PROTESTANT ACCOUNTABILITY TO THE POOR

If Protestantism is to be open to the new possibilities now before us, and if it is not to become something entirely different from what it has been, it will have to accept the notion of accountability to the poor. But it will be a qualified acceptance. It will entail an account-ability to the triune God for the treatment of the poor and for bring-ing to the poor the message of God's love, justice, and hope which is to be incarnated in the midst of life. Protestant understandings of the nature of true faith affirm the power of the Spirit in history, espe-cially among those trapped in involuntary poverty; but they deny that the sources of redemption are to to be found exclusively in his-tory, in material need, or within any single class or movement. The Spirit may well be among the poor, but it is not only there. The fact of poverty and suffering is no more a certain indicator of holiness than is wealth and well-being; and the reasons for wealth or for poverty can seldom be attributed to single factors. Everywhere those who are wealthy are judged by the poor, but Protestants are likely to be less impressed with that human judgment than with the divine judgment that is promised if we ignore the dynamic move-ments of the Holy Spirit and resist the grace that can infuse personal life with a new inner disposition in Christ and bring society under the guiding principles of God's providential will, which demands the constant reform of civilization.

It has been a chief legacy of this whole family of Christian tradi-tions to assert what Tillich calls the "Protestant principle"—the radi-cal notion (more radical even than the legacies of Müntzer, Hegel, Marx, Bloch and proponents of today's Liberation Theology) that nothing immanent can fully possess, exemplify, represent, or be identified exhaustively with the transcendent reality of God. Jesus Christ alone, these traditions confess, was God incarnate. And Christians must seek to ensure that the meaning of the Christ event is incarnated in our personal lives and civilizational structures. But Christ is risen and ascended; we are to conform ourselves to Christ, not to the world. It is true that traces of God's law and purpose can

---

47. See, for examples, Charles H. Kraft, *Christianity in Culture* (Mary-knoll, N.Y.: Orbis Books, 1984); S. Mott, *Biblical Ethics and Social Change* (New York: Oxford University Press, 1982); and Nicholas Wolterstorff, *Until Justice and Peace Embrace* (Grand Rapids: Eerdmans, 1983).

be found in the forms of nature and social history. We betray the Creator when we violate these. But we do so often, and thus nature, society, and history as we experience them are not in themselves adequate guides. Indeed, they may be, must be, reformed on the basis of the right knowledge of God's providential will—as it is discerned above all by Scripture, but also by attentiveness to tradition, reason, and experience (as the *Book of Discipline* of the United Methodist Church so aptly summarizes the belief of most of the Protestant tradition).

In the classic creeds accepted by Protestantism, it is held that the Holy Spirit flows from the first and second persons of the Trinity. Even modern liberal Protestants suggest that the only Spirit that can be called Holy, in distinction from all the spirits that come and go in human historical experience, is to be discerned according to its compatibility with these. Hence the full actualization of the Spirit is, and will remain, beyond history, society, and every movement until the end of time. And the criteria by which we discern which movements of the Spirit are truly Holy as they appear in history, in glimmers and fragments, depend upon transhistorical principles. To deny transcendence in favor of a claim to full immanence is tantamount to idolatry.

Further, major branches of Protestantism—especially in the Calvinist and Puritan traditions—have felt a profound accountability to, and for, civilization. A failure to preserve civilization by continuous, methodical reformation allows its capacity to sustain viable political, educational, familial, cultural, legal, and economic systems to collapse. That impoverishes everyone. Historicist approaches not tied to transhistorical principles that can guide the organizational forms of civilization might be used to deconstruct vicious powers of evil, but they might also destroy patterns of life that are good. And it is doubtful whether they can construct anything viable without being tempted to totalitarian controls. In quite different ways, Lutheranism and modern liberal, democratic Protestantism in the Social Gospel tradition share with Catholicism the notion that civilizational order is something to be preserved.

Insofar as these traditional commitments are challenged or undercut by the new singular accent on accountability to the poor evident among much ecumenical Protestant leadership, it would not be altogether surprising if some Christians would react by gradually coming to approve of magisterial ventures to crush the new heirs of Müntzer with blood and iron as they begin to realize what is at stake in these developments. For what is at stake is not simply a reactionary adherence to ancient dogmas but a deep conviction that key elements of classical Christian teaching, such as the doctrine of the Trinity, are more valid pointers to metaphysical-moral reality than are contemporary epistemologies and philosophies of history. They are also more likely to ensure the relative justice possible in human civilizations than are efforts to understand everything according to a historicized understanding of Spirit. And they are more capable of interpreting and addressing the concrete problems of existence, such as poverty, than are social interpretations based only on class conflict.

And yet, within its own framework of meaning, classical Protestantism has, like classical Catholicism, an insufficiently developed understanding of the Holy Spirit. Earlier treatments of sectarian movements are a present embarrassment, even if it is true that many advocates of the power of the Holy Spirit were a threat to theological and civilizational cohesion. It may well be that the response of magisterial Christians to earlier movements such as that of Müntzer forced those who were caught up in these movements to be cut off, to cut themselves off—doctrinally, ecclesiologically, and socially— from the larger communities of faith.

Today, the spirit of Müntzer lives again, and the deepest question is whether the new awareness of the Holy Spirit can be integrated in a fully trinitarian understanding of God (and God's relationship to humanity), modulating but not destroying or swallowing theocentric and Christological accents, or whether it will break with them once more.

The doctrinal questions are fateful for and symbolic of profound practical issues. Protestantism shares with Judaism and Catholicism (and with many humanist heirs of both the Enlightenment and Romanticism) an ethical conviction that the poor ought not be perpetual losers, that believers ought to embrace, at least in a limited way, the "preferential option for the poor." The embrace is limited in the sense that it is not necessary to accept the analysis of theology, society, and history that many advocates of the idea foment. Indeed, the best allies may be those who challenge untenable claims made by the advocates and try to put the concern for the poor on a more sound foundation. At the same time, Protestants will not view action to overcome poverty and empower the powerless as optional. It is demanded by the triune God and by the nature of evil in human affairs. Reinhold Niebuhr argued again and again what many modern Protestants hold to be the case: while all are equally sinners (the poor being as sinful as the rich), the sins of the rich are more threatening than the sins of the poor because of the greater power that wealth brings. This equality of sin and inequality of guilt demands that Christians side with the weak to constrain the more terrible evils of the powerful.

In contemporary life, this understanding is reinforced psychologically by the widespread shame of affluence. Many who live in relative comfort and who are affected by the gospel do not identify their ease with a sense of being especially blessed by God in contrast to the poor. They reason that God surely did not damn so many to their present condition; it must be human sin that has done so, and we ought to be ashamed if we have not acted to remedy poverty. Those with the wherewithal to change what can be changed have special responsibilities. This psychology confirms for many the doctrinal and ethical arguments being pressed by others and urges them to demand new quests for the best means of remedying systemic poverty. Such are the conditions under which the debate, laced with ambiguity and unclarity, is now being joined in the ecumenical Protestant churches.[48]

It will not suffice, I think, to argue that such reflections are merely ideological masks to protect the political and economic interests of the powerful and rich. If what I have here surveyed is accurate, the issues are rooted in the most profound theological and ethical dynamics of Protestant Christianity. They are unlikely to change unless Protestantism becomes something entirely different from what it has been and is, or unless it dies altogether. Besides, such an argument implicitly denies that religious convictions have any power on their own to shape responses to new challenges, and it implies that those who identify with the cause of the poor are themselves less driven by religious impulses and theological convictions than by their own interests. If that is the case, the interests of the rich will be pitted against the interests of the poor in a power struggle. We do not know who will win, but there is no reason to insinuate religion of any kind into the conflict except as an instrument of power. Protestantism (or any basic religious view) is then emptied of any intrinsic connection to the truth and justice of God and of its capacity to interpret the dilemmas of existence at their deepest levels.

When Tillich asked if we are at the end of the Protestant Era, he

---

48. See Paul Comenisch, "Recent Mainline Protestant Statements on Economic Justice," paper presented to the Annual Meeting of the Society of Christian Ethics, January 1987. Cf. the National Conference of Catholic Bishops' *Economic Justice for All* (U.S. Catholic Conference, 1986); the Committee on a Just Political Economy's *Toward a Just, Caring and Dynamic Political Economy* (Presbyterian Church [U.S.A.], 1985); and the Economics and Theology Group's *Christian Faith and Economic Life* (United Church of Christ, 1987).

seems to have had three issues in mind: (1) the alienation of (especially Continental) Protestantism from the working and oppressed classes, (2) the relative incapacity of Protestantism in its "evangelical" forms to relate constructively to social and cultural life (stressing only the element of "protest" of the "Protestant principle" and failing to encounter anew what he called "catholic substance"), and (3) the incapacity of classical Protestant orthodoxy to make sense to those whose thinking is influenced by thought forms from the Enlightenment and Romanticism.[49] The vibrancy of Liberation Theology and its widespread influence among the leadership of contemporary ecumenical Protestantism invites new reflection on Tillich's first concern.

In the American experience, North and South, Christianity has not been alienated from the masses. Indeed, Protestantism has been largely a movement among the masses—*the* movement, in fact, that has empowered many believers to work their way from poverty to the middle class. In spite of much contempt for middle-class values among the intellectual leadership of Protestantism, populist Protestantism tends to think that everyone ought to be middle class, and that something is wrong (with them or the system) if some are not. They believe that conversion to a disciplined work ethic and the rational transformation of civilization through education, the formation of corporations, and the transfer of technology is the way to improve things.

Many Protestants see in the Liberation movements, particularly in Catholic lands, something of their own history of protest and reform. In spite of notable suspicion about the rhetoric and social theories of these movements, no little quiet glee is felt among many heirs of the sixteenth century that now, in the twentieth, a new evangelical zeal is spreading among the poor and oppressed, who are again thumbing their noses at the pretenses of the Roman Church and developing grass-roots congregations (i.e., "base communities")— although they are tactful enough not to express this glee publicly in an ecumenical age.

There is a growing suspicion, prompted both by misgivings about early Protestantism's intolerant response to the radical sectarian movements and by a current attachment of much of Protestantism to historicism, that a great movement of the Spirit may be afoot. If it is, and we do not attend to it, many fear that Protestantism

---

49. See *The Thought of Paul Tillich* and the papers presented at the International Symposium celebrating the hundredth anniversary of Tillich's birth at Emory University in the fall of 1986 (forthcoming).

will not only petrify, as it did on the Continent, but find that it has been spiritually disobedient to what the sovereign God is doing in history.

The presence of these sentiments suggests that ecumenical Protestantism may be in the process of responding to Tillich's first concern through its engagement in advocacy of the cause of the poor. They have shown no signs of responding to Tillich's second and third concerns, however. Current Liberation Theology is so rooted in a specific metaphysical and epistemological vision of how we are to know the Spirit in history that it considers the divine transcendent only insofar as it is a potentiality of the utopian future, breaking into the present, negating the past, and portended by a messianic class. Such views may assist in breaking the powers of the status quo, but they cannot preserve us from the normlessness of the fluxus quo which they invite. The analysis of history in terms of class conflict is surely one way of understanding poverty, its causes, or its potential cures—or even the nature of social and historical experience more generally—but it is not necessarily the only or chief way. The discovery of history, via Hegel and Marx, may be new to some Protestants, but as Joseph Prabhu, the Third World specialist on Hegel and Marx, put it when commenting on a liberationist paper at the 1986 American Academy of Religion, "It is about time that the churches became more progressive; full speed ahead to the nineteenth century!"

Nor is it clear how ecumenically oriented Protestants who consider liberation the center of faith can give an account of the transcendent truth and justice of God that other Christians claim to be the basis for discerning where, in the midst of life, the tracks of the divine are to be found. A radically immanental historicism tends to undercut the possibilities of a normative theology or ethic that can judge the present contexts of life, guide the reformation of souls and societies, and reckon with perennial political and economic structures of civilizations. It is notoriously hard to discern what the Holy Spirit is doing in history, and all the more so if all transcultural, transhistorical, and transexperiential criteria for discernment are excluded as "unhistorical abstractions" to be overcome. The epistemological foundations of these perspectives are, to say the least, extremely awkward. And if the metaphysical assumptions are correct, it is not possible to demonstrate that they are more valid than their contraries. Why, for example, could it not be said that the rise of fundamentalism in Shi'ite Islam, Theravada Buddhism, Hindu nationalism, and American Christianity shows what God is doing in the world? These "spiritual movements" are as historically powerful as

Christian Liberation movements, and they are taking place among poor peoples of the world.

The question then becomes whether the gospel can combine with the legacies of Müntzer, Hegel, Marx, and the modern revisionists as it did with Greco-Roman, Humanist, and Enlightenment thought at various periods in the past. Could such a new synthesis form a new public theology? Aspects of modern historicism may tend to destroy the very notion that anything transcendent and constant can be real, as earlier partners did not. If this is so, Liberation thought may properly be seen as an important corrective to all religious orientations that use the claims of faith to exploit the poor, and specifically to Protestant theologies that do not include adequate recognition of the power of the Holy Spirit in social history. But such a corrective finds its greatest strength if and when it is itself subject to correction by those forms of personal Christology and by those forms of theonomous regard for the sovereign God who calls to vocation and covenantal discipline. Without this reflexive correction, the capacity of Liberation Theology to aid in the construction of viable Christian social philosophy is doubtful. A theology that centers on the Spirit as it is manifest in history wedded only, or decisively, to a secularized metaphysics and epistemology derived from a historicist interpretation of the Spirit produces only an incestuous dialectic incapable of engendering a hermeneutic of suspicion against its own dangers.

Many ecumenical Protestants (I among them) want very much to be allied with important dimensions of the Liberation movements but simply do not believe that many of the theoretical claims (theological and social-historical) of these new developments are true as they are presented to us, that they are correct in understanding how religions and societies interact, or that they are likely to lead to justice for the poor in the longer run. Movements guided by these claims (and all movements do have to come to major decisions— and repair to governing constituting visions to guide those decisions) are likely either to be tempted to chaos or, in order to prevent chaos, to invite new "totalisms" in civilizations where they succeed in gaining influence.[50]

Müntzer lives again. Protestants, as well as Catholics and evangelicals, have to decide again how to respond. We should not respond exactly as our forebears did. And the Müntzerites of today

---

50. I have attempted to deal with some of these issues in *Apologia: Globalization, Contextualization, and Mission in Theological Education* (Grand Rapids: Eerdmans, 1988).

will also have to decide how to respond to ecumenical perspectives interested in dialogical critique. But more important is the question of whether it is possible to identify standards that can, and should, guide these decisions. For the most part, modern Protestantism is convinced that the classical claims of Christianity provide better, deeper, broader, and finally truer and more just criteria on which to make this judgment and to include selected elements of Liberation thought than does Liberation thought itself. If Protestantism embraces modern historicism without remainder, we shall face difficulties no less severe than those likely to occur if it simply petrifies sixteenth-, seventeenth-, eighteenth-, and nineteenth-century formulas, or those of the twentieth-century Neo-Reformation period, without attentiveness to the possibilities of the Spirit for the future. Should either of these prove to be the case, then we shall have to declare, indeed, that it is "the end of the Protestant era." I, for one, am not yet persuaded.

Option for the Poor: Rethinking a Catholic Tradition

Dennis P. McCann

In his recent book *The Capitalist Revolution*, Peter Berger has argued that if the preferential option for the poor is accepted as the moral norm governing such matters, then "there can be no question that capitalism, as against any empirically available alternatives, is the indicated choice."[1] Berger's conclusion, not surprisingly, echoes the sentiment earlier expressed by the Catholic intellectual Michael Novak, who has affirmed that "the 'option for the poor' *is* the correct option. Everything depends, however, upon the next institutional step," which Novak identifies with a "return to private ownership, to incentives, and to markets."[2] Yet the official pronouncements of the Catholic Church, including the recent pastoral letter of the National Conference of Catholic Bishops (N.C.C.B.) *Economic Justice for All: Catholic Social Teaching and the U.S. Economy*, do not identify the option for the poor with any existing system of political economy. The posture of Catholic social teaching toward capitalism traditionally has ranged from uncomprehending hostility to a grudging acceptance of it as a sinful structure in need of reform.

In what follows, I hope to begin a conversation about the Catholic perspective on the option for the poor in light of the apparently conflicting interpretations represented by Berger and Novak on the one hand and the official expressions of Catholic social teaching on the other. Either Berger and Novak know a thing or two about capitalism that has escaped both the American bishops and those who speak for the papal magisterium or they have failed to grasp what the Catholic Church means by an option for the poor.

---

1. Berger, *The Capitalist Revolution: Fifty Propositions about Prosperity, Equality, and Liberty* (New York: Basic Books, 1986), p. 218.
2. Novak, *Freedom with Justice: Catholic Social Thought and Liberal Institutions* (San Francisco: Harper & Row, 1984), p. 192.

That there legitimately is an option for the poor that is incumbent upon all serious Christians and decent persons regardless of religious orientation is, surprisingly, not in dispute. Though the term itself was originally used by partisans of Latin American Liberation Theology to designate their own distinctive perspective, it has subsequently been adopted by the episcopal hierarchy as a fitting expression of the mainstream tradition of Catholic social teaching. The controversy, in short, is not over whether there is a valid option for the poor but how it ought to be interpreted and implemented pastorally. Paradoxically, then, the option for the poor both unites and divides the church.

In order to get at the meaning of the option for the poor, it is useful to ask what, precisely, the Latin Americans may have had in mind when they called it a "preferential option." I have not been able to document the use of this term prior to its adoption in the "Final Document" produced by the meeting of the Latin American Bishops' Conference (CELAM) at Puebla, Mexico, in 1979. The section devoted to a "preferential option for the poor" comes at the beginning of the fourth part of the document, which outlines a pastoral strategy for Christian witness in the world.[3] It is important to note that this part of the document also includes a "preferential option for young people"; indeed, the document as a whole is studded with any number of pastoral "options," the meanings of which are only partially illuminated by its own description of them as a "choosing process": "This process enables us, after pondering and analyzing both positive and negative realities in the light of the Gospel, to find and adopt the pastoral response to the challenges posed by evangelization."[4] Be that as it may, the plurality of these choices at least suggests a reason why the otherwise redundant term "preferential" may have been accepted by the Latin American bishops. Within their "Final Document" the option for the poor is preferential in the sense that it is more central or enjoys a higher priority than other pastoral options proposed at Puebla.[5]

Gustavo Gutiérrez, the chief architect of Latin American Liberation Theology, holds out for a deeper, more theological interpretation of this preference. In his own commentary on Puebla, he elevates the

---

3. See *Puebla and Beyond: Documentation and Commentary*, ed. John Eagleson and Philip Scharper (Maryknoll, N.Y.: Orbis Books, 1979), pp. 264-67.

4. *Puebla and Beyond*, p. 283.

5. See Archbishop Marcos McGrath, "The Puebla Final Document: Introduction and Commentary," in *Puebla and Beyond*, pp. 87-110.

preferential option to a kind of *imitatio Christi*. Quoting from the working paper that he had written for the Peruvian bishops, he insists that "The privilege of the poor . . . has its theological basis in God. The poor are 'blessed' not because of the mere fact that they are poor, but because the kingdom of God is expressed in the manifestation of his justice and love in their favor."[6] Needless to say, Gutiérrez views the Puebla "Final Document" as a complete vindication of his interpretation. Indeed, he finds in Pope John Paul II's salute to the poor in his address to the barrio of Santa Cecilia—"the pope loves you because you are God's favorites"—further evidence that the preference amounts to a Divine imperative.

This is sheer speculation on my part, but Gutiérrez's claim, as I read it, must be understood in terms of the so-called "fundamental option" that Karl Rahner and his disciples introduced into Catholic moral theology at the time of Vatican II.[7] In his phenomenological investigations of the Christian moral life, Rahner was attempting to highlight the overall tendency or intentionality of a person's life either for or against God, as opposed to the morality of individual actions that had become the dominant focus of ethical reflection among Catholic theologians. Though his elaboration of this concept is consistently formal, it does establish two important points conducive to the development of a preferential option for the poor: (1) it lends authority, among professional Catholic theologians at least, to the jargon of "options," and (2) it provides a basis for understanding the "option" as life's most crucial "choosing process"—namely, the process in which the mystery of one's personal salvation is accomplished. Given Rahner's formal understanding of a "fundamental option," all that is needed to accept Gutiérrez's "preferential option for the poor" is certain substantively biblical convictions about the revelatory authority of the poor as God's favorites in history.

Who, then, are the poor, and why should they be God's favorites? As Gutiérrez insists, they are real people, suffering conditions of material deprivation and destitution. They are the dispossessed, those who have fled the increasingly overcrowded rural areas only to be thrown together with countless others trying to live from day to day in the barrios surrounding the major cities of Latin America. Demographically, they constitute the majority among their fellow citizens; theologically, however, they are identified with

---

6. Gutiérrez, *The Power of the Poor in History* (Maryknoll, N.Y.: Orbis Books, 1983), p. 138.
7. See Rahner, "The Fundamental Option," in *A Rahner Reader*, ed. Gerald A. McCool (New York: Seabury Press, 1975), pp. 255-62.

"the poor of Yahweh," the *Anawim*, who are the first to respond to the biblical hope of salvation. I will assume that these claims are not unfamiliar to you. What needs to be noted here is that this theological identification is ambiguous enough to account for most of the controversy surrounding the option for the poor.

If they are to be counted among the *Anawim*, today's poor must bear a special role in the history of salvation, just as once the *Anawim* were the first to recognize the kingdom of God in Jesus of Nazareth and to have it preached to them. Liberation Theology has been, among other things, an attempt to interpret this special role. Its more rigorous defenders, on this basis, have asserted a "hermeneutic privilege of the oppressed." As Elisabeth Schüssler-Fiorenza has put it, "To truly understand the Bible is to read it through the eyes of the oppressed, since the God who speaks in the Bible is the God of the oppressed."[8] Though Gutiérrez avoids this sort of terminology, he too seems to hold out for such a privilege.

In words that may echo "the scandal of particularity" highlighted in many modern Christologies, Gutiérrez defends the salvific role of the poor:

> Precisely what so many find insupportable in the preferential option for the poor is the claim to announce the gospel within the dialectic of a universality that moves from and through the particular, from and through a preference. But it is precisely this preference that makes the gospel so hard and demanding for the privileged members of an unjust social order. An "exclusivity" would rather leave them on the sidelines, where this proclamation denouncing whatever despoils and oppresses the poor would go right on by them.[9]

Here he is responding explicitly to the remarks made at Puebla by Pope John Paul II, who endorsed a preferential but not an exclusive option for the poor. Though press reports generally interpreted the Pope's words as criticizing Latin American Liberation Theology for its tendency to promote class struggle, in Gutiérrez's view they "actually corroborate precisely what is clearest and sanest in recent Latin American theological experience and reflection." If fact, he is willing to go so far as to say that "From this point of departure it is

---

8. Schüssler-Fiorenza, "Toward a Feminist Biblical Hermeneutics: Biblical Interpretation and Liberation Theology," in *The Challenge of Liberation Theology: A First World Response*, ed. Brian Mahan and L. Dale Richesin (Maryknoll, N.Y.: Orbis Books, 1981), p. 100. Cf. Juan Luis Segundo, *The Liberation of Theology* (Maryknoll, N.Y.: Orbis Books, 1976).
9. Gutiérrez, *The Power of the Poor in History*, p. 128.

possible to proclaim the gospel to *every* human being. Solidarity with the poor, with their struggles and hopes, is the condition of an authentic solidarity with everyone—the condition of a universal love that makes no attempt to gloss over the social oppositions that obtain in the concrete history of peoples, but strides straight through the middle of them to a kingdom of justice and love."[10]

Clearly the option for the poor is no ordinary option for Gutiérrez. It is neither optional nor is it simply a moral imperative. It involves conversion to a substantively theological vision and a serious reexamination of one's way of life. The new vision authenticates itself through solidarity with the oppressed, whose spiritual and moral discernments he accepts as normative for the church as a whole.

Gutiérrez's reassurances, however, were not enough to dispose of the reservations that Pope John Paul II apparently had, in fact, entertained about Liberation Theology and the option for the poor. Almost five years after Puebla, the Vatican issued a document of its own warning against "deviations and risks of deviations, damaging to the faith and to Christian living, that are brought about by certain forms of liberation theology which use, in an insufficiently critical manner, concepts borrowed from various currents of Marxism."[11] Though this document does not repudiate the option for the poor, it does proscribe the use of "Marxist analysis" to create a new hermeneutic that, in the Vatican's view, leads to a "reductionist reading of the Bible." It is the Roman Catholic Church's view, in short, that the biblical portrait of the *Anawim* is not to be used to legitimate modern class struggle within either the church or society; it must not be used as a pretext for a politicization of the gospel.

What the option for the poor might mean apart from such a "deviation" was not fully clarified until the Vatican issued its "Instruction on Christian Freedom and Liberation" more than a year later. In that document, the option for the poor is interpreted as a "preferential love of the poor."[12] The biblical *Anawim* and their special significance in the ministry of Jesus are reaffirmed, and the human misery that normally accompanies material poverty is denounced as "the obvious sign of the natural condition of weakness in which man

---

10. Gutiérrez, *The Power of the Poor in History*, p. 129.
11. Congregation for the Doctrine of the Faith, "Instruction on Certain Aspects of the Theology of Liberation," in *The National Catholic Reporter*, 21 September 1984, p. 11.
12. Congregation for the Doctrine of the Faith, "Instruction on Christian Freedom and Liberation," in *The National Catholic Reporter*, 25 April 1986, p. 42.

finds himself since original sin and the sign of his need for salvation," but the emphasis in this preferential love is clearly upon fidelity to the gospel, understood primarily as the traditional Catholic practice of "detachment from riches" and a "solidarity" based on Christian compassion: "The disciples of Jesus bear witness through love for the poor and unfortunate to the love of the Father himself manifested in the Savior." Lest the point of this exhortation be missed, the document goes on to reiterate the Vatican's rejection of any interpretation of the option for the poor "by means of sociological and ideological categories which would make this preference a partisan choice and a source of conflict."

When one turns from the Latin American discussion to the option for the poor outlined in the U.S. Catholic bishops' pastoral letter *Economic Justice for All*, a similar theological development is apparent. Though the first draft of the letter acknowledges the Latin American bishops' meeting at Puebla as the source of this "option," the meaning of the term has been rendered less confrontational and more universalistic in each subsequent draft, as in the manner of the Vatican's Instructions. Nevertheless, the N.C.C.B.'s contribution is not simply an echo of the previous discussions. The letter develops the option for the poor specifically in the context of contemporary life in the United States, still the most advanced of industrial societies, still maintaining, however precariously, its tradition of democratic pluralism in government and ideology, a nation in which only a relatively small minority can conceivably be regarded as poor or oppressed.

In contrast to the Puebla "Final Document," the bishops' pastoral letter presents the option for the poor not as one pastoral strategy among others but as the moral and spiritual litmus test of a just society. In the letter's final draft, it is typically referred to as "a fundamental 'option for the poor.'"[13] Though the option is interpreted universalistically, and in explicit rejection of views "pitting one group against another," its essential meaning remains substantively theological. It is offered as a fitting expression of the tradition of Catholic social teaching on wealth and poverty:

> Such perspectives provide a basis for what today is called the "preferential option for the poor." Though in the Gospels and in the New Testament as a whole the offer of salvation is ex-

---

13. National Conference of Catholic Bishops, "Economic Justice for All: Catholic Social Teaching and the U.S. Economy," *Origins* 16 (27 November 1986): 411, par. 16; 421, pars. 87-88. Subsequent references to this document will be made parenthetically in the text.

tended to all peoples, Jesus takes the side of those most in need, physically and spiritually. The example of Jesus poses a number of challenges to the contemporary church. It imposes a prophetic mandate to speak for those who have no one to speak for them, to be a defender of the defenseless, who in biblical terms are the poor. It also demands a compassionate vision that enables the church to see things from the side of the poor and powerless, and to assess lifestyles, policies and social institutions in terms of their impact on the poor. It summons the church also to be an instrument in assisting people to experience the liberating power of God in their own lives, so that they may respond to the Gospel in freedom and in dignity. Finally, and most radically, it calls for an emptying of self, both individually and corporately, that allows the church to experience the power of God in the midst of poverty and powerlessness. (P. 418, par. 52)

The emphasis here, as in the reflections of Gutiérrez, is on religious vision rather than specific moral choices. The option for the poor is clearly meant to be imitative of Christ's way of acting. The compassionate vision that it calls for requires imagination and empathy, but it claims no "hermeneutic privilege" for the oppressed.

Having liberated the option for the poor from the hermeneutic difficulties with which some liberation theologians have encumbered it, the U.S. bishops put it to work to establish "moral priorities for the nation." They make of the option for the poor more than just a pastoral strategy for the church, despite its substantively theological premises; in their view, the option makes a moral claim on all Americans. In asserting this, the bishops are not confusing public moral advocacy with evangelization, much less are they abandoning our common commitment to separation of church and state. Precisely because they understand the option for the poor in universal terms as the necessary precondition for a society characterized by "justice for *all*," they are able to urge it upon all citizens as a strategic moral imperative for establishing priorities among various competing principles of social justice as well as the policies that might be warranted by them.

Their advocacy of an option for the poor is best understood in light of the American tradition in Christian social ethics known as the "middle axioms" approach.[14] For our purposes here, it will be

---

14. I have discussed this approach in general terms elsewhere, most recently in collaboration with Charles R. Strain in *Polity and Praxis: A Program for American Practical Theology* (Minneapolis: Winston Press, 1985), pp. 152-69.

sufficient to note that a middle axiom, following the definition of John C. Bennett, is a "guiding principle" that mediates (1) between the specific community of faith in whose traditions it is rooted and society as a whole, and (2) within that community's moral discourse, between "universal ethical principles" and "a program that includes legislation and political strategy."[15] Middle axioms are strategic in that they are contingent upon a particular reading of the historic situation in which the community finds itself. They render otherwise abstract ethical principles provocatively concrete without diminishing our ability to universalize them.

The N.C.C.B.'s version of the option for the poor constitutes a middle axiom not because of anything intrinsic to the option itself but rather because of the framework of moral discourse presupposed in the pastoral letter. Though this framework is less explicit in the final draft of the letter on the economy than it was in the letter on nuclear deterrence (*The Challenge of Peace: God's Promise and Our Response*), it is sufficiently in evidence to help clarify precisely what the bishops do and do not mean by the option for the poor. The framework comprises three distinct but interrelated levels of authority by which the bishops signal the degree of assent that they claim from their diverse readers. The key distinction is between "prudential judgments" on the one hand and "universal moral principles" and "formal Church teaching" on the other.

By "prudential judgments" the bishops recognize the calculus of probability regarding matters of contingent historical fact and interpretation (e.g., the various perspectives of the social sciences) that inform their concrete recommendations for implementing the principles of Catholic social teaching. They ask only a respectful hearing for these "prudential judgments" as morally serious persons wrestle with the concrete practical implications of social justice. No one, not even faithful Catholics, are bound to agree with the bishops when these are at issue. This is not the case, however, with either universal moral principles or formal Church teaching. Universal moral principles, which cover roughly the same field of discourse traditionally governed by so-called "natural law" arguments, are recognizable by all morally serious persons insofar as they are validly asserted and thus are binding upon all. The bishops would place their admittedly controversial doctrine of human rights in this category, for example, and defend it on these grounds. Formal Church

---

15. See Bennett, *Christian Ethics and Social Policy* (New York: Scribner's, 1946); cf. my essay "A Second Look at Middle Axioms," *Annual of the Society of Christian Ethics, 1981*, pp. 73-96.

teaching, finally, is binding only upon Catholics as the living and authoritative expression of the faith of their church. Non-Catholics may subscribe to it or not, but their reasons for doing so are their own and do not necessarily raise *status confessionis* questions as they would for Catholics. Here I place the option for the poor, because it is warranted by substantively theological convictions.

Given this framework of distinctions, how does formal Church teaching function specifically as a middle axiom? Formal Church teaching here is elaborated not in the perennial and abstract terms of universal moral principles, but as a historically situated reading of what Vatican II called "the signs of the times." It makes explicit, if you will, the hermeneutic circle within which the community of faith elaborates its own self-understanding at this particular moment in history. In this sense formal Church teaching does not provide "natural law" argument decked out in appropriately religious rhetoric but rather defines the practical orientation in terms of which the community of faith will make its moral argument in public. In other words, in this framework formal Church teaching mediates between the community of faith and society as a whole and also between universal moral norms and practical programs for implementing these norms.

As Charles Strain and I argue in *Polity and Praxis*, if a middle axiom is actually to mediate in this way, it must be validated as a "generalizable interest." Building on the work of the German social philosopher Jürgen Habermas, we understand generalizable interests as reflecting the authentic aspirations of the community of the faith in a form that the community believes is appropriate for society as a whole. In short, a middle axiom must be regarded as expressing "the *common* interest ascertained *without deception*."[16] Elsewhere I have argued that the theory of generalizable interests provides a useful clarification of the formal intentionality operative in Catholic social teaching on "the common good."[17] Here I must emphasize that without this intentionality, the middle axiom will fail to mediate either between the church and society or between the abstract and concrete dimensions, in this case, of Catholic social teaching.

Seen in this framework, the N.C.C.B. version of the option for the poor is an instance of formal Church teaching validly presented as a

---

16. *Polity and Praxis*, p. 154; cf. Habermas, *Legitimation Crisis* (Boston: Beacon Press, 1975), p. 108.

17. In "The Good to Be Pursued in Common," a paper I delivered at the symposium "Catholic Social Teaching and the Common Good," sponsored by the University of Notre Dame's Center for Ethics and Religious Values in Business, 14-16 April 1986.

middle axiom. The option for the poor mediates between the religious vision of the community and its practical consequences for public morality and social policy. It illuminates the universal moral principles perennially operative in Catholic social teaching by establishing their relevance to this particular moment in the community's history. It provides a context for understanding the prudential judgments that the bishops have made in trying to spell out the practical consequences of this teaching. And it does so precisely because it articulates a generalizable interest. To quote the final draft of the letter on the economy once more, "Those who are marginalized and whose rights are denied have privileged claims if society is to provide justice for *all*. This obligation is deeply rooted in Christian belief" (p. 421, par. 88). What otherwise would seem a strange jumble of religious and secular moral reasoning can here be seen as mediating between the community of faith and society as a whole and making a moral claim upon both precisely because it identifies the common interest ascertained without deception.

Formally considered, that is what I think the American Catholic bishops are up to with their advocacy of an option for the poor. They are defining a moral litmus test for a just society that is both an authentic reflection of the religious vision animating Catholic social teaching and an appropriate expression of our common moral aspirations as Americans. By placing the option for the poor in a framework for public moral discourse, the N.C.C.B. has insured that this fundamental option cannot be construed as an exhortation to class struggle or a politicization of the gospel. Though the final draft of "Economic Justice for All" refers to this framework only occasionally (pp. 425-26, pars. 127-35), it is operative throughout, and in my view, especially in the bishops' discussion of the option for the poor.

While partisans of Liberation Theology may be disappointed by this outcome, the chief result of this formal understanding of the option for the poor is to leave the substantively political question of "socialism vs. capitalism" genuinely open. The N.C.C.B. pastoral letter describes its own approach as "pragmatic and evolutionary" and pointedly refuses to adopt one or another version of systemic analysis that would yield either a blanket condemnation or a legitimation of the U.S. economy (pp. 425-26). One can only conclude that in principle it is possible, in their view, to be either capitalist or socialist while exercising the option for the poor. One's choice of system, assuming that there is a choice to be made, depends on how one reads the empirical indicators of political and economic performance. The choice, in other words, lies in the area of prudential judgments.

Rather than opt for either system, the American Catholic bishops offer an option for the poor as human persons. The pastoral letter, obviously, is not lacking in a certain strategic coherence, but the coherence lies in establishing a participatory ideal of human community that would empower all persons and marginalize none:

> The prime purpose of this special commitment to the poor is to enable them to become active participants in the life of society. It is to enable *all* persons to share in and contribute to the common good. The "option for the poor," therefore, is not an adversarial slogan that pits one group or class against another. Rather it states that the deprivation and powerlessness of the poor wounds the whole community. The extent of their suffering is a measure of how far we are from being a true community of persons. These wounds will be healed only by greater solidarity with the poor and among the poor themselves. (P. 421, par. 88)

There is nothing in the letter suggesting that such solidarity cannot be achieved in a manner consistent with the objectives of a truly democratic capitalism.

At issue between the American Catholic bishops and their critics is not the question of "capitalism vs. socialism" but how to reform the U.S. economy so that it is more supportive of social justice understood in terms of solidarity and participation. The "report" on the pastoral letter recently issued by the so-called Lay Commission on Catholic Social Teaching and the U.S. Economy, while admitting that the letter is "by no means a socialist document," accuses the bishops of advocating in effect "a preferential option for the state."[18] At least one of the bishops' defenders, James Hug, S.J., has responded by accusing the Lay Commission of holding out for "a preferential option for the entrepreneur." What the letter actually suggests is something different from either: a cooperative model of "partnership for the public good" (pp. 440-43, pars. 295-325). What is noteworthy here, however, is that neither the admirers nor the critics of the letter can describe the practical consequences of the option for the poor without reference to some other group or set of institutions.

In the overwhelmingly middle-class reality of American life, spelling out the option for the poor thus involves examining what sorts of coalition building are likely to empower the poor for more effective political and economic participation in our society. The "new American experiment" in economic democracy that the letter outlines in explaining the bishops' view of partnership calls for "cooperation" or collaborative and coordinated economic planning

---

18. Lay Commission on Catholic Social Teaching, "Special Report: Liberty and Justice for All," *Crisis* 4 (December 1986): 7.

at various levels within the economy: within firms and industries and at the local, regional, national, and international levels. The vast majority of the suggestions made here merely involve harnessing the American penchant for voluntary association or networking in ways that will empower people economically and politically from the bottom up. The whole, however, is governed by the traditional Catholic principle of subsidiarity, which "calls for government intervention when small or intermediate groups are unable or unwilling to take the steps needed to promote basic justice" (p. 442, par. 314).

Here, if anywhere, the Lay Commission's protest against "a preferential option for the state" should be considered. The difference between the pastoral letter and the Lay Commission on this issue comes down to a matter of emphasis. As the Lay Commission puts it, "the bishops do tend to lean toward the 'political' in political economy, while experience leads us to lean in the opposite direction. . . . The state must be active, but excessive state entanglement raises barriers."[19] The bishops, on the other hand, consider themselves realists who, while recognizing the considerable amount of economic planning already under way within the U.S. economy, propose that such planning be guided by ethical norms shaped by the option for the poor. Their hope is that experiments in voluntary collaboration will be pursued as creatively as possible; only in the event of continued failure to meet the norms of "basic justice" should the state intervene coercively. In my view this application of the principle of subsidiarity hardly amounts to "a preferential option for the state." Perhaps what disturbs the Lay Commission is the bishops' refusal in the present American political climate to endorse any further deregulation of the economy.

In order to understand what the "new American experiment" does and does not entail, it is useful to think of it in terms of the bishops' discussion of human rights. The "partnership for the public good" outlined in Chapter Four of the final draft of the letter is, in my view, the major strategic recommendation made for fulfilling these rights more effectively in the U.S. political economy. The doctrine of human rights reviewed in the letter has proved to be very controversial, for it goes beyond the civil and political rights guaranteed by the U.S. constitution to assert certain basic economic rights: "As Pope John XXIII declared, all people have a right to life, food, clothing, shelter, rest, medical care, education and employment. This means that when people are without a chance to earn a

---

19. Lay Commission on Catholic Social Teaching, "Special Report," p. 7.

living and must go hungry and homeless, they are being denied basic rights" (p. 411, par. 17).

Surprisingly enough, the Lay Commission challenges this assertion not on the grounds that it constitutes a departure from traditional American thinking about human rights, but rather on the grounds that it constitutes a distortion of papal teaching. They maintain that Pope John's teachings do not extend these rights to all persons but only to "those who are unable 'through no fault of [their] own' to meet their responsibilities to provide for themselves and their dependents" (Pacem in Terris, no. 11; emphasis added). Were the Lay Commission's reading to stand, the bishops ought to make a sharp distinction between "welfare rights," to which those who fail through no fault of their own are entitled, and "economic rights," which protect economically "activist individuals and their associations."[20] Economic rights, in this view, would concern the conditions necessary to make each family self-reliant—notably, private property and decent working conditions.

What Pope John XXIII actually wrote, however, tends to support the N.C.C.B. interpretation. His words deserve to be quoted in full:

> Beginning our discussion of the rights of man, we see that every man has the right to life, to bodily integrity, and to the means which are suitable for the proper development of life; these are primarily food, clothing, shelter, rest, medical care, and finally the necessary social services. Therefore a human being also has the right to security in cases of sickness, inability to work, widowhood, old age, unemployment, or in any other case in which he is deprived of the means of subsistence through no fault of his own.[21]

Contrary to the Lay Commission, Pope John does not restrict the right to "the means which are suitable for the proper development of life" only to those who are deprived of these means "through no fault of their own." A right to "security" is added to the list to cover such cases, but this right provides merely a social warranty for those unable to secure these basic rights on their own.

Admittedly, when the American Catholic bishops elaborate this right to the means suitable for personal and social development in a package of "economic rights," they are going beyond the exact

---

20. Lay Commission on Catholic Social Teaching, "Special Report," p. 10.

21. *Justice in the Marketplace: Collected Statements of the Vatican and the U.S. Catholic Bishops on Economic Policy, 1891-1984*, ed. David M. Byers (Washington: United States Catholic Conference, 1985), p. 152.

wording of this papal encyclical. Nevertheless, their terminology is well grounded in the current pope's encyclical *Laborem Exercens* and is certainly faithful to the spirit of Pope John XXIII's remarks. The American bishops defend their terminology, especially the "right to employment," because, as they indicate in a footnote, "the ordinary way people earn their living in our society is through paid employment." Hence their conclusion that "the protection of human dignity demands that the right to useful employment be secured for all who are able and willing to work" (p. 449n.39). The Lay Commission's assertions to the contrary notwithstanding, this is anything but a misreading of papal teaching.

A more useful avenue of criticism is opened up by the Lay Commission's question concerning whether these social warranties are appropriately designated as "rights." With good reason, the Lay Commission fears that "in our highly legalistic society, it is dangerous to speak of rights without exact clarity."[22] Their point is that rights here are understood as legal entitlements that the state must fulfill regardless of the consequences. This fear, I contend, is what influences their view that the pastoral letter is offering "a preferential option for the state." The bishops, on the other hand, are insisting on the integrity of their own use of moral terms. For them, as for the mainstream of Catholic social teaching, rights are primarily moral rights the fulfillment of which is the duty of each person in particular and society as a whole. Consistent with the principle of subsidiarity, such moral rights require state intervention only when these duties cannot be fulfilled on any other basis. This clarification, of course, does not really address the Lay Commission's fear of confusion, for the confusion at bottom involves a conflict of cultures. The best the bishops can do in the pastoral letter is pledge themselves to undertake an educational effort to develop a "new cultural consensus" (p. 421, par. 83). Without this effort, of course, there is little hope that their "new American experiment" will actually yield the anticipated partnerships for the public good.

If, as I believe, the bishops can consistently allow "room for diversity of opinion in the church and in U.S. society on *how* to protect the human dignity and economic rights of all" (p. 421, par. 84), then it is clear that the proposed "new American experiment" involves a greater degree of flexibility in implementing these rights than the Lay Commission apparently envisions. I do not want to collapse the logical distinction in ordinary moral language between "rights"

---

22. Lay Commission on Catholic Social Teaching, "Special Report," p. 9.

(deontological) and "goals" (teleological), but short of that mistake, it seems that the bishops certainly do not envision the fulfillment of "economic rights" as some sort of unconditional imperative. The right to employment, for example, clearly does not entail that no worker can ever be fired for good reasons or laid off because of economic conditions affecting the firm as a whole. Nor has the right to private property in Catholic social teaching ever been regarded as absolute. Moral rights exist in a reciprocal relationship to moral duties, and both, apparently, exist in some sort of dialectical tension with the common good. Indeed, though the bishops could have emphasized this point more forcefully, there are trade-offs to be faced in fulfilling various economic rights, and between economic rights on the one hand and political and civil rights on the other. The "new American experiment" is not constrained to fulfill these economic rights in a manner that would jeopardize the basic viability of the American economy. Rather, the fulfillment of these rights is contingent upon our capacity to optimize the efficient use of the limited resources available to us, a goal that the bishops understand is determined by the current state of our politics and technology, among other things. In emphasizing "economic rights" as forcefully as they do, the bishops have put us on notice that in their view we are not managing as well as we could, at least when judged according to the norms of "basic justice."

There is one other matter that merits attention before we conclude this review of the American Catholic bishops' "fundamental 'option for the poor.'" The pastoral letter denounces the current inequalities in the distribution of wealth and income in this country as morally "unacceptable" (p. 430, par. 185). There are problems in this section of the letter and, not surprisingly, it has been criticized rather persuasively in the Lay Commission's report.[23] Though it asserts a contrary intention, the bishops' letter conveys the impression of a bias in favor of economic egalitarianism. It would be difficult if not impossible to reconcile such a bias, were it actually proven, with the bishops' acceptance of the "mixed economy" of American capitalism as the framework for their moral deliberations. Nevertheless, I would argue that a careful reading of the letter indicates no such bias, though occasionally their remarks are a source of confusion.

The key to disentangling their teaching on economic inequality lies in asking what, if anything, constitutes the basis of their moral concern: is it inequality as such or is it the feared impact of current

---

23. Lay Commission on Catholic Social Teaching, "Special Report," pp. 12-13.

levels of inequality upon our nation's capacities to exercise an option for the poor? At stake here is their central notion of human dignity as involving social solidarity and participation. The bishops' only legitimate moral interest in patterns of wealth and income distribution hinges upon whether current levels of economic inequality make it impossible for some citizens to participate effectively in the life of our society as a whole. Even assuming that no one is denied the means of subsistence, if some people in fact are marginalized politically and socially because of their unequal share in the nation's wealth and income, then such inequality is legitimately regarded as a "moral scandal." It must be remedied as soon as possible up to the point where marginalization ceases to be a problem. But over and above that point, if the bishops are consistent, they really should have no public moral concern about the distribution of wealth and income. In this view, then, what separates—and ought to separate—the bishops from their critics on the Lay Commission is their moral judgment not on distributional inequality as such but on the growing disparity between the nation's rich and poor over the past decade and its apparently subversive effect on our capacities for genuine social solidarity and unrestricted political participation. Were their differences to be narrowed to this point, then the bishops' discussion of wealth and poverty would be seen more clearly as consistent with the overall interpretation of the option for the poor that the pastoral letter offers.

My attempt to rethink Catholic social teaching as an option for the poor has been informed by more than just the previous conversations with the Latin American bishops and theologians involved in producing the "Final Document" at Puebla or with the American Catholic bishops' pastoral letter *Economic Justice for All*. As I indicate in the introduction to this essay, in the back of my mind I have also been dialoguing with Peter Berger's recent work *The Capitalist Revolution*. Much can and ought to be said about Berger's propositions and the option for the poor. I, for one, prefer Berger's analysis of capitalism to that of Michael Novak in *The Spirit of Democratic Capitalism*. Berger is to be commended for at least once having had the good sense to leave the theologizing to the theologians! Be that as it may, potentially Berger's most constructive contribution to the Catholic discussion of an option for the poor stems from his distinction between capitalism as an economic system and the larger anthropological process that he describes as modernization. Much of the animus of Catholic social teaching against capitalism can be attributed to the church's ongoing and largely unacknowledged struggle with modernity.

Let me develop this point briefly in relation to another Catholic discussion, this one in *Option for the Poor: A Hundred Years of Vatican Social Teaching*, a book by the Irish missionary Donal Dorr. The subtitle of this work suggests that Dorr is trying to impose a teleology on Catholic social teaching that is neither warranted historically nor advisable politically. Dorr, of course, is too careful a scholar simply to equate the option for the poor with the traditional thrust of papal social teaching, but he would like somehow to leverage the option's authority by establishing a certain continuity. The teleology that results, alas, makes a critical dialogue over the prospects for a capitalist option for the poor less, rather than more, likely.

In light of Berger's distinction between capitalism and modernity, however, it is possible to look again at the larger tradition of Catholic social teaching going back all the way to its quasimythological origins in Pope Leo XIII's *Rerum Novarum*. Dorr is right to see this paradigm of the modern papal social encyclical primarily as protest. What he fails to emphasize sufficiently is the extent to which Leo XIII was a paternalistic reactionary whose social thought had yet to come to grips with the realities of modern industrialization. All Pope Leo could see was the pain of the obvious social dislocations and all he could do in response was denounce them. His view of the motives of those who were agents for change was reductive and thoroughly negative. This is not to deny that "greed" in some cases was in fact the real problem, but it is clear that the Pope was unable to understand capitalist development on any other basis.

So modern Catholic social teaching begins as the sincere protest of a dispossessed Italian prince unable to come to terms with the final disappearance of a feudal, agrarian society even in Central Europe. Pope Pius XI's *Quadragesimo Anno*, which appeared at the height of Italian fascism, actually does confront the emerging industrial society, but it does so in a typically Central European form. Were it not for fascist encroachments upon the church's traditional social prerogatives, the defense of which required the Pope to devise a stopgap "principle of subsidiarity," the solidaristic alternative to capitalism and communism outlined in that encyclical would be virtually indistinguishable from the social and economic program that Mussolini actually sponsored.

The possibility of a legitimately democratic capitalism begins to surface in Papal social teaching only during and after World War II. It is not farfetched to attribute Pius XII's accommodation to the victorious Western allies to the geopolitical necessities of postwar Central Europe. Christian Democrats, as both the Pope and the Allied commanders knew, were the only hope for staving off the political triumph of communism. I could rehearse the story down to the pres-

ent, but it would be tedious to do so. The point is that Catholic social teaching, for all its idealism, has been as lacking in a critical
appreciation of the virtues of modernity as has been Catholic dog-
matic theology, ecclesiology, and biblical scholarship. The Church of
Rome, despite the intellectual and spiritual renascence of Catholicism in the postwar North Atlantic community and its momentary
triumph at Vatican II, for the most part of the last century has been
in reactionary revolt against modernism, intellectually and politically, religiously and socially.

Measured by this account, the American Catholic bishops' option for the poor is breathtakingly modern, for although a residue of
the traditional Catholic animus surfaces here and there in the letter,
for the most part—as I read it—it signifies a critical acceptance of the
ethos of democratic pluralism and its likely economic expression in
capitalism. Read in this light, very few are the propositions offered
by Peter Berger that the American Catholic bishops would take exception to. There would be problems, I suspect, with Berger's analysis of the "new knowledge class," but on the whole I think the bishops would welcome, for example, Berger's historical and
comparative analysis of patterns of wealth and income distribution
in relationship to the processes of modernizing industrialization.

Would the bishops then agree with Berger that, judged by the
norm of an option for the poor, "capitalism, as against any empirically available alternatives, is the indicated choice"? For the moment, I think not—not because they disagree fundamentally with
Berger's analysis but because they understand the option for the
poor differently. Given their own unresolved ambivalence about
modernization, they would hold out for more than the elimination
of "certain types of material misery." What that something more actually entails in terms of systemic social change they never quite
spell out. But surely it is an expression of the religious vision animating the option for the poor and is manifest in their continual reference to human dignity and to a just society characterized by genuine
solidarity and unrestricted participation. Inasmuch as these
possibly utopian ideals themselves are a legacy of the Catholic reaction against modernity, perhaps it is just as well that the bishops finally refuse to identify the option for the poor with any economic
system. The *tercerismo* all too typical of Catholic social teaching, in
the bishops' hands, thus may turn out to be a useful *via negativa* for
the American social imagination.

The Preferential Option for the Poor and American Public Policy

Robert Benne

I. INTRODUCTORY AFFIRMATIONS

A. Theological Considerations

The evidence that God has a bias toward the poor runs throughout the biblical narrative. The election of Abraham, the liberation of Israel from the bondage of the Egyptians, the prophetic insistence on justice for the poor, and the teachings and ministry of Jesus all point to God's particular concern for the poor. From the very beginning to the present, the history of the church has manifested a continuing care for the poor, sick, and homeless.

But the central thrust of Christian concern for the poor follows as a response to the love shown toward humans by God in the salvatory event of Jesus Christ. In the life, death, and resurrection of Jesus Christ a particular kind of love—agape—reaches out to reconcile a fallen humanity. So the Christian confession goes.

This redeeming love, received in faith, is to become active in service to and care for the neighbor. Christians are to love others as Christ has loved them: that is the new commandment. The qualities of agape shown by God toward humanity are to be reflected in some way in the Christian life. Such a calling is the center, in terms of motivation and vision, of the Christian concern for the poor.

Christian ethicists such as Anders Nygren and Reinhold Niebuhr have delineated the qualities of agape.[1] It is disinterested: it initiates love without guarantee of return and without assessing the "value" of the beloved. It is universal: it encompasses all beings with equal

---

1. See Nygren, *Eros and Agape* (London: SPCK, 1957); and Niebuhr, *An Interpretation of Christian Ethics* (New York: Meridian Books, 1958), pp. 43-62.

regard. It pushes the lover beyond the personal to the social and political spheres of life. At the same time, it is strategically aimed at the least, the lost, and the vulnerable—not because they deserve to be loved more than others but because their need is greater. Further, agape aims at the true good of the other, not the good and righteous feelings of the lover who bestows love. It aims to invite the other into active, centered mutuality with other persons and activities. Finally, this outgoing love will often be suffering love in a fallen world, for the resistant sin of this world will often reject or take advantage of it. The cross of Christ is a reminder for the Christians of the hazardous nature of agape. Besides the difficulties of expressing this radical love in social or political circumstances, which we shall discuss presently, there are pitfalls in even the personal expression of agape. Anything as sublime as agape is vulnerable to distortion. As Reinhold Niebuhr insightfully observes, only things of great allure or value are compelling enough for people to idolize or pervert. Agape is no exception. People can become so infatuated with their own agapeistic motives or ideals that they neglect to focus on the good of the one who is loved. In such instances, givers may fix recipients in dependent relationships or treat them permissively—that is, fail to hold them accountable to mutual obligations of created existence. In either case, agape becomes an instrument of negation.

A further distortion of agape occurs when it is claimed, as some advocates of Liberation Theology claim, that God loves the poor to the exclusion of others, particularly the wealthy. And sometimes the universal principle gets in the way of loving particular persons— especially those whom familiarity has rendered objects of contempt. Finally, the outgoing character of disinterestedness and the willingness to suffer can lead to the doormat-of-the-world syndrome wherein one isn't happy unless one is either a loser or a martyr.

Nevertheless, in spite of these distortions, the vision of agape draws the Christian toward service to the poor and others who need healing. It is a reflection of the divine love that reconciled a separated world to itself. It participates in the rescue mission of God to retrieve a lost creation, a creation that will wend its way to hell without the healing power of agape. Love reaches out to invite mutuality, which is the original intent and possibility of worldly life that has been frustrated by sin.

There are two basic obstacles to the Christian challenge to express agape in the public sphere. The first and most common is the disinclination of many Christians to do so. They limit their love to those close at hand, offering it only in the personal sphere of face-to-face encounter. They regard the world beyond the personal as subject to another law—"business is business" or "politics is politics."

They resist the universalizing propensity of agape and split life into the personal and the social. Some theologies (e.g., perversions of the Lutheran two-kingdoms approach) have given theoretical legitimation to such bifurcation. But many Christians do not feel the need to justify theoretically their inclination to limit their love to the personal. They just act that way.

A second obstacle is the tendency to attempt to express Christian love *directly* as public policy. This is a weakness of the "children of light," who genuinely want the poor to be lifted up. This approach is characterized by an insistence that disinterestedness, a bias toward the poor, universality aiming for the other's good, and a willingness to suffer be ensconced directly in public policy. Put another way, it proposes that the radical ethic of agape become a direct guiding principle for public policy and, for that matter, other kinds of worldly activities, such as business and international relations.

This misplacement is most often made by liberal Christians. For example, J. Philip Wogaman recently asserted that because as sinners we are equally justified by God's grace and love rather than our works, so "economic good should be produced and distributed in such a way as to enhance human well-being . . . without asking first whether people have deserved what they receive."[2] Sometimes the mistake is made from the right, as when George Gilder suggests that love is the motive behind the search for profit in a free-market system.[3] In neither case is the transcendent quality of agape taken seriously. In the latter, love is made to fit easily with obvious self-interest. In the former love becomes a direct possibility for guiding policy. In any event, the dangers that accompany the personal expression of agape are multiplied greatly in the area of public policy. Policies keep their recipients dependent or fail to hold them accountable. The poor are idealized so much that we are prohibited from any criticisms of them. Or no serious consideration of effects is countenanced if loving but inappropriate motives are demonstrated.

A proper theological ethic itself must protest a direct use of love in public policy. Indeed, such a sustained protest was one of Reinhold Niebuhr's primary missions as a theological commentator. Niebuhr argued that love can be only indirectly relevant to politics and economics. It must be mediated by middle principles such as justice and order that take into account the sin and finitude of the world. Those principles—if effective in policy—aim at holding

---

2. Wogaman, *Economics and Ethics: A Christian Inquiry* (Philadelphia: Fortress Press, 1986), p. 35.

3. Gilder, *Wealth and Poverty* (New York: Basic Books, 1981), p. 262.

people accountable for specific and limited responsibilities, consider soberly the persistent self-interest in persons and groups, and respect the capacities in society's natural equilibrium for self-correction. At the same time, just principles embodied in public policy go beyond charity in that they are guaranteed by law rather than by the less reliable impulses of generous people.[4]

The "world," too, demands a distinction between love and public policy. Mickey Kaus, writing in the *New Republic*, polemicizes against the easy use of the word *compassion* in current political discussion. "The aim of liberal government should be not to increase the incidence of compassion, but to reduce the opportunity for it," he says. "Charity is a noble impulse. But it is not the relation of free equal citizens."[5]

Hannah Arendt also worried about the role of love (pure goodness, compassion) in the public sphere. It tends, she said, to "abolish the distance, the worldly space, between men where political matters are located."[6] Love generally remains politically irrelevant, but where it does press its relevance into the political sphere it unleashes violence by inviting those driven by necessity (survival, hunger) into political action.

We are arguing, then, that the Christian motivation and ideal of agape derives from the central events of the Christian drama of redemption and that such love is the basis for service to the poor but that it must be expressed in public policy indirectly through principles and practices *that are fit for the world*. Those principles and practices, because of their worldliness, will share common ground with principles and practices advocated by other persons of good will. They will be open to discussion and debate on the basis of broader criteria than that of Christian love, though from a Christian point of view they must have some affinity with the direction of Christian love. As principles "fit for the world," they will participate in all the ambiguities of this complex and fallen world. There can be no claim that their successful implementation is salvatory in the religious sense of the word.

B. The Political-Economic-Social Context

If a Christian preferential option for the poor is to be expressed in a

---

4. See Niebuhr, *The Nature and Destiny of Man*, vol. 2 (New York: Scribner's, 1949), pp. 244-60.

5. Kaus, "Up from Altruism," *New Republic*, 15 December 1986, p. 30.

6. Arendt, *On Revolution* (New York: Viking Press, 1963), p. 81.

way fit for the American world, it will be worked out in our system of democratic capitalism. American government, with the consent of the people and with limits placed on it by the Constitution, will instigate public policy, but it will do so in the context of complex and intimate relations with the market economy and the pluralist social system that are its partners in the American experiment.

We need not argue whether this democratic capitalist world *ought* to be the context for a preferential option for the poor, though an increasing number of secular (Kristol, Gilder, Friedman, Hayek, Berger) and religious (Novak, Heyne, Neuhaus, Benne) arguments have been made for precisely that arrangement. The simple fact is that American democratic capitalism *is* the system within which public policy with regard to the poor will have to be forged in the future, as it has been in the past and is now. There will be no radical shifts in this arrangement in the short or medium terms, partly because of the inertia of any massive social system but also partly because it has performed satisfactorily enough to be affirmed by the vast majority of people. As Peter Berger has argued, democratic capitalism "has created a wealth of 'facticities'—economic and social facts, that to a large extent, have come to be taken for granted and thus legitimate themselves."[7]

Many religious liberals ignore this point to their peril. When they detect serious challenges within the system of democratic capitalism, they call for vast changes that resemble the democratic socialism they prefer. For example, the Catholic bishops, after assessing the amount of poverty in the United States, called for "fundamental changes in social and economic structures."[8]

Furthermore, it seems clear that if we were considering only the long-term prospects of the poor, we could stop at this point and simply say, Let the system proceed. Despite its flaws and its short-term, localized setbacks for the poor, the democratic capitalist system will improve the prospects of the poor rather dramatically over the long haul. Again, Berger, pulling together many empirical studies on this issue, observes that "there can be no question that capitalism, as against any empirically available alternatives, is the indicated choice."[9]

---

7. Berger, *The Capitalist Revolution* (New York: Basic Books, 1986), p. 208.

8. National Conference of Catholic Bishops, *Economic Justice for All: Catholic Social Teaching and the U.S. Economy*, 3d draft (Washington: U.S. Catholic Conference, 1986), p. 51.

9. Berger, *The Capitalist Revolution*, p. 218.

But our concern here is with the capacities of public policy to alleviate the plight of the poor in the short and medium run—in the next ten to twenty years. After all, as Lord Keynes noted, in the long run we are all dead. So the question becomes how we are to pursue a preferential option for the poor through a public policy fit for this particular world in the short to medium range.

A brief answer—to be expanded shortly—is that public policy must pursue justice for the poor in ways that move *with* the gifts, values, and inclinations of American democratic capitalism rather than against them or in a manner oblivious to them. This approach takes seriously our criterion of fitness for the world, since those gifts, values, and inclinations have been legitimated by persistent practice. They have come to terms with the human limitations and possibilities of the American people. More substantively, the approach I am proposing combines a liberal conception of justice with the conservative values of decentralization and efficiency. This neoliberal project aims at liberal goals pursued with conservative means. These three core values are deeply embedded in American practice: the liberal conception of justice stems from our political tradition, decentralization from our pluralist socio-cultural disposition, and efficiency from our pragmatic economic orientation. The great public policy challenge before us is to improve the prospects of the poor through policies that are just, efficient, and decentralized.

C. The Significance of Mood

Besides the persisting system of democratic capitalism, there are seasonal moods that add important limits and possibilities to public policy initiatives. I believe there are two relevant moods in the present situation. The first could be captured by the phrase "tight-fisted times," especially with regard to the possibility of major new domestic programs. Our mounting federal budget deficit, trade imbalance, foreign debt, and interest on the national debt combine to make massive new domestic policies unlikely. The Gramm-Rudman legislation will most likely force cuts in all programs, even the military. A preferential option for the poor will have to be exercised within sharp restraints. New programs will have to be replacements for old ones and cost only marginally more or, better, roughly the same. Cost effectiveness will be very important.

The Catholic bishops' pastoral letter on the American economy recommends programs that would entail massive new amounts of money. It suggests that some money for the initiatives could be gained by diminishing the military budget.[10] But it does not realistically face the constraints of a necessarily tight-fisted time.

A second element of national mood is not so limiting. To the contrary, it presents a new opening for improving the prospects of at least certain groups among the poor. It is a change in perception regarding the causes and cures of poverty. For some time there was a focus on external factors of discrimination and other forms of active oppression on the part of the surrounding society as the major source of poverty; that focus is now shifting to the internal resources of a person or community as crucially important.

This mood is a far cry from the days in the late sixties when Daniel Moynihan was lambasted for his work on the disintegrating black family and Edward Banfield was shouted down on major university campuses for citing class culture as a strong variable in social mobility. Both were charged with "blaming the victim," and the whole effort to place at least some responsibility for poverty on poor persons or communities was sharply rejected. It seemed clear to the great majority that the problem had to be located in oppressive society.

Things have changed. Commentator after commentator has recently stressed that the habits, skills, and moral virtues of persons and communities are just as important as external factors—both negative and positive—in making one's way in life. Columnists (Raspberry), economists (Sowell), journalists (Kaus), and political scientists (Mead) have argued that the formation of practical and moral agency in the poor is one important route to betterment.[11]

There is a growing awareness that the problem is far more difficult and complex than just active oppression of the poor. As Edward Banfield argued many years ago, even if we were able to wave some magic wand and take away all the external problems that impede some of the poor, the central characteristics of what he called "lower-class culture" would remain.[12] We now call people mired in such culture the "underclass." And it is that group—by no means

---

10. National Conference of Catholic Bishops, *Economic Justice for All*, p. 79.

11. See William Raspberry, "Some Better Ideas on Welfare," *Roanoke Times and World News*, 9 December 1986, p. A11; Thomas Sowell, *Ethnic America* (New York: Basic Books, 1981); Mickey Kaus, "The Work Ethic State," *New Republic*, 7 July 1986, pp. 22-33; and Lawrence Mead, *Beyond Entitlement: The Social Obligations of Citizenship* (New York: Free Press, 1985).

12. Banfield, *The Unheavenly City* (Boston: Little, Brown, 1970), pp. 43ff.

the only or even largest segment of the poor—that provides the greatest challenge for public policy directed toward the poor.

D. The Poor

There are obviously many kinds of poor people among the 33 million encompassed by the government's official definition.[13] Appalachian hillfolk, unemployed steelworkers, children of poor families, bankrupt farmers, the urban homeless, teenage welfare mothers, unemployed and often unemployable minority youth, drug addicts, a portion of the elderly, and people with very low-paying jobs come to mind as examples. And filling each category are human beings struggling to survive and to wrest some small meaning and pleasure from their lives.

But perhaps the most tragic among all these are the *children* of the underclass. The underclass is that group of low-income Americans, numbering about nine million, that exists on the edge of society and is associated with much of the crime, welfare dependency, and illegitimacy that have come to afflict American life in recent decades.[14] The underclass lacks the necessary internal resources—habits, skills, character, discipline—to be attractive enough for employers in the market economy to hire. They have little to contribute to the legitimate economy and it therefore rewards them meagerly, if at all. A significant portion of the underclass is made up of female-headed households in which illegitimacy is common, if not normative.

It is the children of such "families" that seem to me to call out most convincingly for whatever preferential option for the poor we can muster. Without effective help, their chances of escaping the underclass are slim. Without help they are likely to reproduce similar "families," thereby increasing the misery of the poor.

It is to this group—the children of the underclass—that I wish to respond later with a public policy proposal. Obviously this is but one group among many to which policy must be addressed. But since it is impossible to suggest specific policies with regard to even the major groups needing attention, I will turn instead to suggesting a general approach that can serve as a guide for shaping policy of various sorts. I think it combines the values of justice, decentraliza-

---

13. This figure is cited in *Economic Justice for All*, p. 47.
14. See Ken Auletta, *The Underclass* (New York: Random House, 1983).

tion, and efficiency in ways that can make a preferential option for the poor fit for the world.

II. MIDDLE PRINCIPLES

If love calls Christians to adopt a preferential option for the poor as they help in shaping public policy, it must work through mediating principles that take into account the reality of the world. Love, I would argue, must aim at extending justice to the poor in ways that are decentralized and efficient.

A. Justice

Love demands that we ask ourselves as *citizens* what we owe our fellows, and especially the poor. Since we cannot love our fellow citizens directly, some conception of justice must answer the question. In spite of all the objections that have been raised against the scheme John Rawls elaborates in his *Theory of Justice*, I believe it is the most persuasive elaboration of justice for our pluralistic, liberal tradition. True enough, his hypothetical original position dehistoricizes people, his principles are formal and cannot handle certain substantive moral issues, and he is too concerned about equality of condition. Nevertheless, with some modifications, I believe the principles to be eminently useful. So the approach I'm about to outline can fairly be called Rawlsian, although it is not slavishly so. How can Rawlsian principles embody a Christian preference for the poor?

1. *Liberty.* First, we owe our poor brothers and sisters the same right to participate in electing those who govern us as other citizens. Efforts to make voter registration easy and accessible to the poor are a high priority. The votes of the poor are one of the major means they have for insisting that society respond to their interests.

Second, the civil liberties of the poor must be guarded. They must be treated as citizens are meant to be treated—as ends in themselves and never solely as means. The bundle of negative freedoms that is the pride of liberal democracies must be guarded for the poor, in spite of the temptations to intervene directly in the lives of the underclass. Shortcuts to improve the lot of the poor must be avoided if they violate civil liberties. Coerced sterilization, abortion, or arbitrary removal of children from parents are unacceptable, for they directly violate liberal traditions of justice as well as Judeo-Christian notions of respect for persons.

Conversely, however, the poor should themselves be held accountable to their obligations of citizenship. Moreover, a judicious use of incentives and disincentives does not constitute a violation of liberties. Indeed, as Charles Murray has argued, government has often arranged incentives for the poor that have tended to erode individual responsibility and family life.[15] The issue is not whether incentives are acceptable; it is rather what kind of incentives are used and to what ends. Later I will propose what I consider to be a proper use of incentives with regard to education for the poor.

Economic and political conservatives often limit their conception of justice to this first principle. In a memorable exchange with Walter Williams in which I tried to come up with obvious cases of hardship for which we commonly assume the government ought to be responsible, he interjected impatiently that the only thing we owe each other besides respecting our liberties is economic opportunity, and the market provides that!

To this truncation of justice Rawls has an admirable response. The impoverished may have liberty, he says, but their liberty lacks worth.[16] They do not have the economic or social wherewithal to exercise the freedoms they have. Freedom of access to the housing market doesn't have much worth if one has no money to rent or buy accommodations. Political and civil liberties are foremost and precious in our tradition, but they do not exhaust our obligations to each other as citizens or as Christians who are also citizens.

2. *Fair equality of opportunity.* Equality of opportunity means that positions are filled by those who can perform the requirements of the position, that applicants are selected on the basis of proper criteria. This part of the principle rules out racial, ethnic, and sexual discrimination. Fortunately, recent public policy has moved a long way in diminishing such discrimination. It is extremely important that we continue to extend antidiscriminatory policies toward the poor, especially the racial minorities among them. They do not need the insult of discrimination added to the injury of poverty.

It should be noted that equality of opportunity aims at a fair game or race; it does not try to fix the results. Policies that promote fair employment have been injured by qualifications that fix the results through quotas. Quotas may be necessary for the most intransigent of those who resist fair employment, but they should be used exceedingly sparingly. They inevitably bring resentment and feel-

---

15. Murray, *Losing Ground* (New York: Basic Books, 1984), pp. 154ff.
16. Rawls, *A Theory of Justice* (Cambridge: Harvard University Press, 1971), p. 204.

ings of unjust treatment, even among the supposed beneficiaries of such approaches. An injustice must be very great indeed before quotas will be a lesser evil.

The more challenging component of fair equality of opportunity concerns the modifier *fair*. Rawls rightly sees that many of the poor are severely disadvantaged in even a nondiscriminatory system of open positions. Persons from well-off backgrounds have acquired skills and habits from their nurture that enable them to compete adequately for open positions. *Fair* equality of opportunity entails helping to move those who are disadvantaged closer to the same line that the relatively advantaged are starting from in the competitive race.

Certainly one of the most important public policy initiatives, particularly for the children of the underclass, has been the provision of child care and training for the very young. Head Start, for example, has proven to be quite effective in getting the children of the poor closer to the starting line. That federal program should by all means be continued and extended. But it need not be the only vehicle of providing care and training for the children of the poor.

Peter Berger and Richard John Neuhaus have suggested that public programs should be supplemented by mechanisms that would facilitate the entry of the private nonprofit sector into the provision of such care and training, an approach that "was embodied in the Mondale-Brademas bill which President Ford vetoed in 1976. As in the Head Start Program, this plan would work through prime sponsors. These sponsors would be private or public, voluntary associations, neighborhood groups, or simply parents getting together to run a day care center—the only condition being that sponsors be non-profit in character."[17] Such a system would not only provide a fairer equality of opportunity, but it would do so in a *decentralized* way. Moreover, it would effect the third in our triumvirate of values, *efficiency*, by using a voucher system to ensure a modicum of choice and competition in the provision of a needed service to the poor.

> The voucher approach can be the more readily used in day care since there are not as yet in this area the powerful vested interests so firmly established in primary and secondary education. Vouchers would facilitate day care centers that are small, not professionalized, under the control of parents, therefore highly diversified. State intervention should be strictly limited to financial accountability and to safety and health standards

---

17. Berger and Neuhaus, *To Empower People* (Washington: American Enterprise Institute, 1977), p. 24.

(which, perhaps not incidentally, are absurdly unrealistic in many states). Considerable funds can be saved through this approach since it is virtually certain that economics of scale do not apply to day care centers. Imaginative proposals should be explored, such as the use of surrogate grandparents—which, incidentally, would offer meaningful employment to the growing numbers of elderly persons in our society.[18]

Even if youngsters have a better beginning in life and more equal chances in schooling, it will do little good if they do not have adequate opportunities for subsequent job training and employment as well. In these areas it would be wise to rely basically on the for-profit sector. Business enterprises are more accurate in their judgment about what jobs will be extant in the future and are more disciplined and efficient in their training processes. Vouchers and subsidies should be made available to the young of the underclass who seek training and jobs. At the same time, minimum wage laws should not be applied for persons under twenty-one. This, in combination with subsidies for training and employing disadvantaged young people, would encourage enterprises both large and small to employ more of the young.

These stratagems would give the children of the poor a fairer start—that is, they would partly compensate for the disadvantaged conditions of their early nurture. But fair equality of opportunity as a principle of justice is a chimera unless our market economy is producing a wide variety of jobs. As the Catholic bishops recognize, a better shake for the poor is dependent on the growth of the economy.[19] But again, relatively unfettered market economies such as that in America seem to be much more efficient in creating jobs than are the more encumbered European economies.

3. *A social minimum.* Rawls calls this the "difference principle," but to my mind he joins the Catholic bishops in being too concerned with equality of condition. He calls for transfer systems that will maximize the prospects of the poor as the general living standard advances—and he does so as a way of justifying continuing inequalities in the social system, as if equality is the natural human state of affairs and is only skewed by injustice.[20] It seems to me that inequality is a stubborn fact of life and does not need to be justified or eradicated. However, I would like to argue that love seeking justice in an affluent society will aim at policies that guarantee all mem-

---

18. Berger and Neuhaus, *To Empower People,* pp. 24-25.
19. See *Economic Justice for All,* p. 53.
20. See Rawls, *A Theory of Justice,* p. 75.

bers a social minimum. We owe each other a safety net, to use the common parlance. We should be more concerned about serious suffering than about inequalities.

Only real curmudgeons argue that those clearly unable to contribute to the economy—the seriously handicapped, the impoverished elderly, the orphaned, those immobilized by catastrophic illness—should not be supported by transferring wealth to them from us. Indeed, from a Christian point of view, the Rawlsian "maximin" interpretation with regard to this group makes a good deal of sense. How we treat this group is certainly a touchstone of how just we are, and no doubt we can do better here, particularly if we can encourage the private nonprofit system of mediating institutions to play a larger part.

An important proviso with regard to helping the poor purchase critical goods and services in the economy is that it is generally far better to give direct subsidies to the poor for housing, fuel, medical care, and the like than to erect public policies that fix prices in the market. This latter option is often proposed by liberal groups, particularly religious groups, who fail to see the long-term consequences of their proposals. For example, rent control inevitably creates shortages of housing for the poor and benefits the well-off who can afford to pay more for their housing. It is much wiser to enable the poor to purchase what they need at the going market rate.

The more ambiguous issue with regard to a social minimum has to do with able-bodied poor adults. Until recently a large share of commentators, following a wide spectrum of economists, have favored a negative income tax as a way of supplying a minimal cash income while at the same time providing incentives to work.

While still attractive, this approach has been criticized at several points. First, it is unlikely to do much to clear away the cultural pathology of the underclass, although it would be an important aid to those who are willing to work in the legitimate economy. Second, even if its payments were at a minimal level, it could encourage continued dependency. Third, it does not honor the reciprocity between the rights and obligations of citizenship; if society guarantees any sort of social minimum, it should at the same time require a reciprocal contribution of some sort.

Enter the challenging proposal of theorists such as Mickey Kaus and Lawrence Mead. Consonant with the mood change mentioned earlier, both writers argue that the internal orientation of the underclass is a key variable in its immobility. They agree with conservatives that it is culture, not politics, that determines the success of individuals and communities in society. But Kaus is no conservative. He believes that public policy can change a culture and save it from itself. After criticizing a number of workfare schemes, he proposes his own.

> What is required, I think, is something like this: replacing all cash-like welfare programs that assist the able-bodied poor (AFDC, general relief, Food Stamps, and housing subsidies, but not Medicaid) with a single, simple offer from the government—an offer of employment for every American citizen over 18 who wants it, in a useful public job at a wage slightly below the minimum wage. If you could work and needed money, you would not be given a check and then cajoled, instructed and threatened into working it off or "training it off" (workfare). You would be given the location of several government job sites. If you showed up, and worked, you would be paid for your work. If you didn't show up, you don't get paid. Simple.[21]

Kaus goes on to defend his proposal from a host of possible objections. All in all, it is a very persuasive approach toward a "work-ethic state" that would begin to transform the dependent culture of the underclass. It moves beyond the "Alexandrian solution" of Murray and the cynical despair of Banfield, neither of which offers much constructive hope. However, it certainly violates one of the elements of mood we discussed earlier—namely, the resistance to large new domestic programs. Kaus thinks the populace could be persuaded to support his proposal because of its affirmation of the work ethic. Perhaps so.

But a modified form of this proposal made by Lawrence Mead seems even more promising, and it avoids both huge new federal outlays and the criticism that government administration of millions of jobs would be chancy at the least. Indeed, Mead's modification honors the three values of justice, decentralization, and efficiency.

He suggests that the government provide private-sector job and/or training, search, and placement services. It could also provide some jobs at low pay as a backup. At any rate, the able-bodied poor would be required to work or prepare for work in the ordinary jobs that most other Americans do every day. The cost of training for those jobs and salaries for working in them would then be supplemented by the current earned income tax credit or by the innovative wage rate subsidy system advocated by Robert Lerman. But the

---

21. Kaus, "The Work Ethic State," p. 30.

point would be that support would come only for those that work or prepare for it.[22]

I hope that the policies I have proposed in this lengthy discussion of the middle principle of justice are indirectly connected to the Christian ideal of love on the one hand and the stubborn limits and vibrant possibilities of American society on the other. Certainly there are distinct echoes of Christian love in respecting the agency of every individual (liberty), in treating persons with equal regard (fair equality of opportunity), and in programmatically assisting and supporting the most disadvantaged (social minimum). And I think each policy takes into account the limits and possibilities of this particular "world," a subject to which I will now turn directly.

B. Decentralization

I have already made use of the principle of decentralization in suggesting concrete policies in the preceding section. I would now like to add some general reflections concerning it.

The idea here is to use our vast and variegated private sector as the vehicle of services to the poor, even though the government might be the guarantor of those services. Certainly one of the major characteristics of American society is its profusion of active and healthy private organizations, both nonprofit and for-profit.

There are many reasons why private-sector organizations are a highly appropriate means of delivering goods and services to the poor. First, since there are many of them in "competition" with each other, they provide choices for the poor that government monopolies do not. Second, such organizations—especially the nonprofit ones—tend to be smaller and are less likely to be plagued with struggles between contending bureaucracies. They are often closer at hand to the poor, so that meaningful participation is more likely. Third, they are autonomous: they can and are constrained to make their own decisions in the light of their values and their realistic limits. Fourth, these organizations are often connected with communities of vision and virtue. They have a value-laden practice that imparts moral direction and discipline. Incidentally, it is very important that public policy not leech out through regulation the particular character of the services provided by these historical communities.

---

22. See Mead, "Not Only Work Works," *New Republic*, 6 October 1986, p. 21.

A mark of wise public policy is use of the decentralized private sector as extensively as possible. Government should step in to provide direct services to the poor only as a last resort, though in many cases it should underwrite and regulate at a minimal level the private agencies that do deliver them.

C. Efficiency

The value of efficiency comes primarily from the economic sphere, though it also tends to be inherent in the operation of the pluralist, decentralized social system just discussed. Private-sector organizations must be efficient in order to survive.

Efficiency in its economic sense assumes scarcity. The factors of production are scarce, while the desire for goods and services is unlimited. Efficiency means that those scarce factors must be combined in effective ways to produce goods and services at the lowest price possible for those willing and able to pay. Alas, government agencies have not been held rigorously to the demands of efficiency in the past. But there is increasing awareness that government indeed has limits and that public policy must be efficient. This will mean, I believe, that we will have to cut back on middle-class entitlements if we are to take seriously our obligation to the poor. Gov. Richard Lamm of Colorado, for example, has made an eloquent argument for means tests for very expensive entitlements such as Medicare, Social Security, veterans benefits, and "heroic" medical care for the elderly.

Efficiency also demands taking a hard look at effects and consequences, not simply intentions. Charles Murray has raised powerfully the question of effects with regard to our current welfare policies, concluding that good intentions have led to ill effects. There is little doubt that to some extent this is true, although activist religious groups resist a sober consideration of effects and persist in supporting well-intentioned but often permissive and inefficient social policies.

Finally, and very importantly, efficiency demands respect for and proper use of self-interest in shaping public policy. This criterion seems obvious, but in fact it is rarely employed properly. Either self-interest is relied upon totally, as in various libertarian public policy proposals, or it is ignored completely, as in many liberal—particularly religious-liberal—proposals. Libertarian-leaning theorists such as Milton Friedman believe that a negative income tax scheme will lead the underclass right out of their dependency by appealing to rational self-interest. But will it? Perhaps self-interest will simply lead people to accept as much as possible without being lured into work. Libertarian proposals on the use of school vouchers also assume that the poor will be as quick as the middle class in exercising their self-interest by selecting quality schools for their children.

On the other hand, liberals tend to be oblivious to the factor of self-interest among the poor. Well-intentioned liberal programs often arrange incentives that produce effects that are precisely the opposite of what was intended because they do not account adequately for self-interest. With regard to this point, Murray argues persuasively that the current welfare system encourages the poor to act in their short-term rather than long-term advantage (by discouraging entry into the labor force and maintenance of a stable family life).[23]

III. A MODEST PROPOSAL

It is widely known that Milton Friedman, followed by a number of libertarians, has been keenly interested in eroding the near monopoly on primary and secondary education held by the public school system. He proposes that the state give a voucher worth a year's education to parents for each child of school age. The vouchers would be nontransferable but could be used in public or private schools. They would expand the choice of parents and force public schools to compete on equal footing with private schools.[24]

Many telling criticisms of this proposal have been made, and not just by those who are defensive proponents of the present system. Chief among them is the objection that middle-class parents would quickly move their children into private and parochial schools on their vouchers, that those schools would fill up, and the children of disadvantaged families would be left with the public schools, which would become dumping grounds for the worst cases. This is a convincing criticism. But what if the families of disadvantaged children (children of one-parent families below a very low income level) were given vouchers worth 150 percent of the cost of a year's education? Private and public schools could arrange education to appeal to those children because there would be an incentive to do so. Catholic and other church-related schools would have an advantage because they have had a lot of practice in such arrangements. Many

---

23. See Murray, *Losing Ground*, pp. 154-77.
24. See Friedman, *Capitalism and Freedom* (Chicago: University of Chicago Press, 1962), pp. 175-87.

poor families could then afford such educations, and the schools could afford to give it to them. Church schools could offer a more disciplined context that could emphasize moral values. They could tap the idealism of many young people, who in turn would be able to make a living teaching the disadvantaged and would also be more inclined to do so in environments that were healthful and effective. Meanwhile, the public schools would have to compete for their clients. Poor parents would have a choice. Both public and private systems would reach out to the poor.

The worth of vouchers for private education could be scaled against family income, while vouchers for public education could be worth the full amount as a minimum. This would give incentives for middle-class parents to keep their children in public schools. But all across the board choice would be real and effective. This would not only break down the monopolies that presently help to block improvements in urban education but would open important educational channels for the poor.

In many small-town and suburban areas, such schemes would not be necessary, since disadvantaged children already have access to the same schools that more advantaged children attend. But in those areas where the poor have miserable opportunities, such an approach might be tried. Several state legislatures have similar plans before them, among them the state of Minnesota.

IV. CONCLUSION

There is good news and bad news. The good news is that both neoliberals and neoconservatives seem to be converging in their social analysis and policy prescriptions. The creative edge of analysis and prescription takes seriously the values I have recommended—justice, decentralization, and efficiency. Neoliberals seem to have jettisoned the old liberal penchant for advocating constantly expanding universal entitlements with their attendant danger of permissiveness and dependency, for choosing public agencies as the main or sole vehicle for delivering services to the poor, and for allowing good intentions to blind them to the negative effects of their policies. Neoconservatives seem to be expanding their thin notions of justice and reaffirming their commitment to private-sector efficiency and decentralization. Christian laypeople are deeply involved in both "neo" movements, motivated by love for the poor and attempting to shape a scheme of justice fit for the world. There are great obstacles to their success, but there is hope.

The bad news is that there seems to be cultural lag in the

churches, particularly those of the Protestant mainstream. While well-intentioned, they seem to cling to the old liberal agenda, unchastened by the serious flaws of the old ways. They have not yet been mugged by reality, and that prevents them from being active participants in an exciting new movement that may augur a better day for the poor.

To Throw Oneself into the Wave: The Problem of Possessions

Gilbert Meilaender

The Christian Scriptures provide no single rule governing attitudes and actions in the realm of possessions. Perhaps for this reason, "the church has always been more hesitant to lay down a rule of practice about money than it has . . . about sexual relations," even though the destructive power of possessions is every bit as great as that of sexuality.[1] There may also be reasons more general in character why we should be reluctant to universalize any single view of possessions as *the* Christian view, a point to which I will return later. But we can begin to think about the problem of possessions by juxtaposing a few biblical texts.

I

Blessed are the poor in spirit, for theirs is the kingdom of heaven.

Matthew 5:3

Blessed are you poor, for yours is the kingdom of God.

Luke 6:20

These passages—and the contrast between them in their Matthean and Lukan forms—are well known. Taken together they raise a question. Who are the poor upon whom God's blessing—life in the kingdom—is bestowed? Is God's favor shown to all the poor in spirit, all who know themselves to be beggars before him—who, even when they have done all that is asked of them, say, "We are unworthy servants; we have only done what was our duty" (Luke 17:10)? Or is God's favor shown particularly and preferentially to

---

1. Philip Turner, *Sex, Money and Power* (Cambridge: Cowley Publications, 1985), p. 90.

those who are poor in the goods of this world, those who, like the beggar Lazarus, long for the crumbs that fall from the tables of the wealthy—but who, when they die, are carried by the angels to Abraham's bosom (Luke 16:19ff.)?

If God's favor is to be understood as preference for those who are poor in the things of this world, the case will have to be made elsewhere than from the Old Testament. For the Hebrew Scriptures also recognize the ambivalence to which the Matthean and Lukan forms of Jesus' beatitude point. Israel's God is one who

> raises the poor from the dust,
> and lifts the needy from the ash heap. (Ps. 113:7)

But the Israelite sage knows that there is another kind of poverty cutting more deeply into the human soul.

> It is better to be of a lowly spirit with the poor
> than to divide the spoil with the proud. (Prov. 16:19)

And at the most fundamental level of human "being," our material condition cannot affect our relation to Israel's God.

> The rich and the poor meet together;
> the LORD is the maker of them all. (Prov. 22:2)

In the Old Testament there is condemnation of those who oppress and show no concern for the poor, but there is little condemnation of wealth itself.[2] After we have finished calling attention to prophetic woes uttered upon the rich who trample the poor, and after we have taken note of the legal provisions connected with the year of jubilee, we will still have to grant that the legitimacy of possessions is both presupposed and protected by the Decalogue's commandments forbidding theft and covetousness. Radical poverty is not an ideal. The prophetic picture of the day when all peoples come to Zion can be described in terms of a settled life of moderation and contentment once experienced under Solomon: "They shall sit every man under his vine and under his fig tree" (Mic. 4:4; cf. 1 Kings 4:25).

It is therefore something genuinely new when Jesus says, "Blessed are you poor, for yours is the kingdom of God." New and powerful—but not to be taken alone. It does not mean that the gospel's invitation is addressed primarily or exclusively to those who are poor in this world's goods—"the poor, the maimed, the lame, the blind" (Luke 14:13). We must read this blessing together

---

2. See Martin Hengel, *Property and Riches in the Early Church* (Philadelphia: Fortress Press, 1974), pp. 12ff.

with the expression of God's favor toward all who, like the tax collec-
tor, say, "God, be merciful to me a sinner" (Luke 18:13). Such poverty
of spirit frees one from the bondage of both poverty *and* wealth.

Even in Luke's Gospel, with its special attention to the poor and
lowly, the relation to God is fundamental. If Luke does not cite Jesus'
saying about the first and greatest commandment—love of God—
he nonetheless teaches the lesson in a striking and profound fashion.
In chapter 10 he recounts Jesus' story of the Good Samaritan—the
story which, perhaps more than any other, has powerfully depicted
the requirement of love especially for the neighbor in need. Yet, that
is followed immediately by the brief account of Jesus' visit to the
home of Mary and Martha. This is the Jesus who has just pointed to
the Samaritan and said, "Go and do likewise." And when Martha attempts in her own way to do likewise, to serve the needs of Jesus
while Mary sits contemplatively at his feet and listens, he says to
Martha: "One thing is needful. Mary has chosen the good portion . . ." (Luke 10:42). That poverty of spirit is asked of every person—rich or poor—and is the one thing needful.

If the church is to be an agent of reconciliation among all who are
poor in spirit (even if, perhaps, rich in this world's goods), its calling
must be chiefly, though not exclusively, to speak the good news of
Christ and to let its faith be active in works of mercy. That offer of
God's favor to all who are poor in spirit, even though it may not
directly address the most immediate needs of the poor, can never be
irrelevant to the human condition. The church's vision must always,
in Reinhold Niebuhr's terms, discern the equality of sin underlying
the inequality of guilt in human life.[3] What is at stake here is chiefly
a question of emphasis, of centrality in the church's mission. For
surely it is true that, in addition to speaking the word of the gospel
and letting its faith be active in works of love, the church is to let its
love seek justice through words of witness. But when the *central* element in the church's mission becomes partisan advocacy in the
political arena, "the evangelistic voice of the church is muted. . . .
Even though political activity is mandated by love, it masks love's
face in a way that evangelism and direct care of the poor do not."[4]

The church risks irrelevance, in fact, when it makes central in its
vocation God's preference for the poor and not his universal favor
toward the poor in spirit. For a partisan God, whom we can enlist in
political struggle, is a God we can capture and possess. And we may

---

3. Niebuhr, *The Nature and Destiny of Man*, vol. 1 (New York: Scribner's, 1964), pp. 219ff.
4. Turner, *Sex, Money and Power*, p. 92.

wonder whether, when the day comes that such a God is no longer useful as a means toward our partisan ends, we will not find the message of his favor to have become irrelevant.

II

> Do not lay up for yourselves treasures on earth, where moth and rust consume and where thieves break in and steal, but lay up for yourselves treasures in heaven, where neither moth nor rust consumes and where thieves do not break in and steal. For where your treasure is, there will your heart be also.
>
> Matthew 6:19-21

> Either make the tree good, and its fruit good; or make the tree bad, and its fruit bad; for the tree is known by its fruit. . . . The good man out of his good treasure brings forth good, and the evil man out of his evil treasure brings forth evil.
>
> Matthew 12:33, 35

Luke Johnson suggests that when we seek a theological understanding of the proper place of possessions in our life, we should focus primarily on motivation, the chief determinant of Christian character. "We are convinced that our identity is found in our inner heart, where we desire and will, and that God, the discerner of hearts, looks not so much to our actions as to our intentions."[5] From this perspective the problem of possessions is chiefly a problem of getting from "in here" to "out there"—achieving the right attitude, a righteous inner self, so that this self may handle external goods properly.[6] And yet, despite this emphasis, Johnson must grant, a few pages later, that the direction of movement also goes the other way—from "out there" to "in here," from external things to inner self. The way we dispose of external things not only expresses the self we are but also forms and shapes that inner self.[7] Inner spirit is expressed through external structures—and, indeed, a right inner spirit can probably be expressed through a variety of structural arrangements. But structure also shapes spirit, and anyone concerned for inner virtue cannot ignore the formative influence of the things we use and possess.

---

5. Johnson, *Sharing Possessions* (Philadelphia: Fortress Press, 1981), p. 31.
6. Johnson, *Sharing Possessions*, p. 32.
7. Johnson, *Sharing Possessions*, pp. 36-37.

We have not exhausted all there is to be said about the Christian life when we have discussed motives and noted that a good tree will bring forth good fruit, for it is also true that our hearts will be shaped by the location of our treasure. Christians have not usually wanted to say, for example, that an inner motive of life would suffice to sanctify any and every sexual act. Because we are embodied spirits, the disposition of the body (and not simply motive) counts morally. Some bodies are already committed in sexual relationships. Some cannot enact the union of those who are other, as male and female are other. There is no reason why structure should not also count when we turn from the issue of sexuality to that of possessions.

The problem of relating spirit and structure does not arise solely when we reflect upon wealth and poverty; it is a perennial difficulty for Christian living. Because *structure shapes spirit*, moral virtue is simply habit long continued. The inner self—what we are likely to call "character"—is developed and molded by the structures within which we live daily. Only gradually do we become people whose character is established—who, for better or worse, can be depended upon to act in certain ways. All of us believe that structure shapes spirit to this extent. If we did not, we would pay far less attention to the social environment in which we—and others, such as our children—live. Although possessions are not bad, they are dangerous. They can corrupt the spirit: "where your treasure is, there will your heart be also." But *spirit cannot be reduced to structure*. We cannot guarantee a virtuous inner self by rightly ordering structures. We may give away all that we have, even sacrifice our life, and yet—so the apostle tells us—"have not love" (1 Cor. 13:3). Just as God cannot be captured or possessed by our side in any partisan struggle, so true virtue cannot simply become our possession—as if the mysterious working of God's grace on our inner self had no part to play, as if the tree did not have to be made good before its fruit could be good.

III

"One thing you still lack. Sell all that you have and distribute to the poor, and you will have treasure in heaven; and come, follow me." But when he heard this, he became sad, for he was very rich. Jesus looking at him said, "How hard it is for those who have riches to enter the kingdom of God! For it is easier for a camel to go through the eye of a needle than for a rich man to enter the kingdom of God." Those who heard it said, "Then who can be saved?" But he said, "What is impossible with men is possible with God."

Luke 18:22-27

It would be hard to find a story from the New Testament that has had a greater impact upon Christian history than the story of the rich ruler who came to Jesus with high hopes for discipleship and left sorrowfully, clinging to his possessions. "One thing you lack," Jesus says. And generations of Christians, called to what they thought of as special religious vocations, have heard in these words a counsel of perfection—a possibility for Christian living that goes beyond the careful use of possessions required by the commandments. Others have labored with sincere diligence to interpret the passage in ways that made clear that the camel Jesus had in mind could indeed squeeze through the eye of the needle he had in mind. This story, in fact, has all the ambiguity we have noted in the sets of passages discussed above.

We can learn a good bit by considering the story through the eyes of Clement of Alexandria, a Christian philosopher who lived at the beginning of the third century in a city that had become a center of learning, culture, and wealth. Not all Christians who came to him for advice were necessarily prepared to sell all that they had and distribute it to the poor. Nor did Clement think they should. His essay "The Rich Man's Salvation" is a thoughtful and instructive discussion.

Clement notes that what Jesus chiefly asks of his followers (and what he really wants from the rich ruler) is that they rid themselves of the passion for wealth and the anxiety this passion breeds. In speaking to the rich man, Jesus does not, Clement writes, "bid him throw away the substance he possessed, and abandon his property; but bids him banish from his soul his notions about wealth, his excitement and morbid feeling about it, the anxieties, which are the thorns of existence, which choke the seed of life."[8] And if we are likely to think that Clement strains a bit too much in suggesting that Jesus does not bid the young man to abandon his possessions, it is still true that on the essential point he is very near the mark. The danger, Clement believes, lies not simply in external possessions but in the inner spirit of passionate desire for goods. Things themselves he considers neutral; what counts is how we use them, the attitude we adopt toward them. "For it is no great thing or desirable to be destitute of wealth" (p. 94). Clement will not grant that simply being without earthly goods, being destitute and a beggar, makes one

---

8. Clement of Alexandria, "The Rich Man's Salvation," in *Christian Ethics: Sources of the Living Tradition*, ed. Waldo Beach and H. Richard Niebuhr (New York: Ronald Press, 1973), p. 94. Subsequent references to this work will be cited parenthetically in the text.

"most blessed and most dear to God" (p. 95). On the contrary, he is persuaded that what God is concerned with—and what Jesus was aiming at in his advice to the rich ruler—is a right inner spirit. "It is not the outward act which others have done, but something else indicated by it, greater, more godlike, more perfect, the stripping off of the passions from the soul itself" (p. 95).

This is Clement's basic interpretive move. Possessions themselves are entirely neutral; it is spirit, not structure, that concerns God. What counts is not what we have but how we use it. And yet, he himself realizes that the issue is more complicated than this. What we have *may* affect who we are—possessions may shape character. Clement notes this in a rather backhanded way. Having argued that there is nothing particularly holy about lacking wealth, that we might give away all that we own and still be consumed by the passion for things, he suggests that it might even be dangerous *not* to possess any of this world's goods. "For it is impossible and inconceivable that those in want of the necessaries of life should not be harassed in mind, and hindered from better things in the endeavour to provide them somehow and from some source" (p. 95). Having too little may lead to anxiety and concern—may corrupt the inner spirit. The insight here is not unlike that of the Israelite sage:

> Give me neither poverty nor riches;
> feed me with the food that is needful for me,
> lest I be full, and deny thee,
> and say, "Who is the Lord?"
> or lest I be poor, and steal,
> and profane the name of my God. (Prov. 30:8-9)

What this must mean, however, is that things, and the way we structure and possess things, are not entirely neutral. It is, I suppose, not entirely surprising that the point should come through in so "backhanded" a way in Clement. His audience would not be sorry to hear that there might be dangers in *not* possessing. But if there are dangers in poverty, if possessions therefore are not simply neutral, we will have to conclude in turn—what Clement does not note— that there may also be dangers in possession and acquisition.

To see this is not to undermine Clement's central point; indeed, it may be to reinforce it. For, although possessions are not simply neutral, what is clearest is that no particular way of possessing *or* not possessing can guarantee a spirit of trust in God alone for our security. The ideal for life that emerges in Clement's discussion seems at first, therefore, to be one of *moderation*. The acquisitive passions of the soul should be controlled and moderated. To the degree they achieve this, Christians will neither be distressed in times of adversity nor led astray by the seductions of wealth.

There are, however, hints in Clement of an ideal that goes beyond that of balance and moderation. It is possible, after all, that the life of moderation might be largely self-serving. Clement does not entirely forget that Jesus asks something harder of his followers. The ideal is not simply a pure, temperate inner spirit; rather, that spirit is sought at least in part because of the action to which it will give rise. Followers of Jesus should have possessions without clinging to them—*so that* they are always ready to give to those in need. "For if no one had anything, what room would be left among men for giving? . . . How could one give food to the hungry, and drink to the thirsty, clothe the naked, and shelter the houseless, . . . if each man first divested himself of all these things?" (pp. 95-96).

To come this far with Clement is to see again the ambivalence of Christian thought about possessions. How shall we describe the proper attitude as Clement depicts it? We might say: moderate your desires *and* be ready to give to those in need. And yet, at any moment—or every moment?—that readiness to give might reach down and begin to transform the measured tones of one's moderation. It might seem that about at least one thing—giving to the neighbor in need—the Christian should be *im*moderate. There is no place for mediocrity in such service. Clement himself writes that the Christian knows he possesses goods "more for the sake of the brethren than his own" (p. 98). Where will such an *im*moderate spirit of giving lead? Back to Jesus' words, "sell all that you have and distribute to the poor"? Clement does not, of course, mean for that to happen. But to see it reemerge, even as a possibility, from Clement's discussion is to see why Christian thought has been unable to say only one thing about possessions.

We can distinguish at least three attitudes, each of which takes root in the soil of Christian faith.

1. Possessions are both a dangerous threat and a good opportunity. To avoid the dangers, we need the virtue of *simplicity*—to choke off the passion for things and moderate our desires. To seize the opportunities for service, we need the virtue of *generosity*.[9]

2. Regularly seizing the opportunity to give to those in need may call for and give rise to something more than a moderation of our desires; it may suggest the need for *renunciation*. Clement writes to oppose this move, and he is surely correct to see that not all Christians are called to such a life—correct also to see that this is no higher

---

9. Turner, *Sex, Money and Power*, pp. 88-90.

way, since it can offer no guarantee of a purer inner spirit. What Jesus
says to the rich ruler is the precise truth: *no one* is good but God alone.
But Clement's own case suggests—almost against his will—that the
way of renunciation may be the way some Christians must go.

3. An attempt to practice the virtues of simplicity and generosity
may give rise to a sense of *tension* within the Christian life—tension
that pushes the whole of that life in a relatively *austere* direction. Pre-
supposing the possession of goods, the virtue of generosity seems
(like Clement) to call simply for a right inner spirit and by itself sets
no limit (other than the neighbor's need) to what we possess. Pre-
supposing the danger of possessions, the virtue of simplicity re-
minds us that things are not simply neutral. Too much—though also
too little—can corrupt the soul. The call for simplicity is essentially
a reminder that we are seldom as generous as we think, as we could
be, as we ought to be. The call for generosity is essentially a reminder that the desire to live a simple life is not the same as the
desire to help those in need; it can be largely a self-serving desire.
We may, for example, retreat from the life of society; we may choose
subsistence for ourselves. But in doing so we are retreating from a
life of exchange and interdependence into one of autonomy and in-
dependence. The virtues required of us stand in some tension. "Civilization is commanded, yet civilization can safely be practised only
by those to whom it is promised that 'if they drink any deadly thing
it shall not hurt them.'"[10] Yet, the virtues of simplicity and generosity need not and will not simply stand in tension within the Christian life. They will often be complementary and, when taken seriously, will together transform the whole of life in a relatively austere
direction—a direction perhaps concealed in the "and" by which we
held together Clement's two emphases: be moderate in desires *and*
desire immoderately to help the needy.

For such a life of moderation and austerity there are, however, no
universalizable rules. The way of renunciation is not a higher form
of Christian life than that of simplicity, and simplicity is not always
to be preferred to the wealth that makes possible greater generosity.
"One of the marks of a certain type of bad man," C. S. Lewis once
wrote, "is that he cannot give up a thing himself without wanting
everyone else to give it up."[11] At issue here is the nature of Christian
vocation. Room must be left for freedom of the Christian life—and,
perhaps still more, freedom of the God who calls Christians to dif-

---

10. C. S. Lewis, "Williams and the Arthuriad," in *Arthurian Torso*
(London: Oxford University Press, 1948), p. 134.
11. Lewis, *Mere Christianity* (New York: Macmillan, 1960), p. 62.

ferent ways of life.[12] Beneficence to others in need is a duty for Christians, but the ways in which that beneficence may be enacted are many, and no single way can be universally required. Luther offered the following explanation in his *Small Catechism* of the commandment prohibiting stealing, for example: "We should fear and love God that we may not take our neighbor's money or goods, nor get them by false ware or dealing, but help him to improve and protect his property and business." Luther here first articulates a negative prohibition that admits of universalization: no one should take another's goods or get them through deceit. But the positive norm, the beneficence required—to help the neighbor "improve and protect his property and business"—can be enacted in countless ways that love may find but the moral law can neither specify nor require. But since such beneficence must ultimately flow from "fear and love" of God, the problem of possessions is, finally, a problem of trust.

IV

> There is more simplicity in the man who eats caviar on impulse than in the man who eats grape-nuts on principle.
>
> G. K. Chesterton

> Man, please thy Maker, and be merry,
> And give not for this world a cherry.
>
> William Dunbar

Such virtues as contentment, simplicity, temperance, justice, generosity, and hospitality are important. And such vices as greed, avarice, covetousness, envy, and ambition are—because of their destructive power—important. But at the heart of our attachment to things is the need for security. In what or whom do we place our confidence? To say that our life consists not in what we possess but in our relation to God, not in the goods we have compared to what others have but in the affirming verdict of God upon our lives, is not to say that the things of this world are of no importance. But it does make the issue of trust central.

In *Perelandra*, one of his space fantasies, C. S. Lewis explored this theme—the role played by trust in shaping our attitude toward created things. The protagonist of the story, a man named Ransom,

---

12. For a more detailed argument, see my essay "Is What Is Right for Me Right for All Persons Similarly Situated?" *Journal of Religious Ethics* 8 (1980): 125-34.

is taken to the planet Perelandra—a newly created world of almost indescribable beauty. He finds himself in "a part of the wood where great globes of yellow fruit hung from the trees."[13] Since the juice of an unknown fruit might not be healthful for a human being, he intends to take just a small experimental sip, but at the first taste he forgets such caution. "It was like the discovery of a totally new *genus* of pleasures, something unheard of among men, out of all reckoning, beyond all covenant. For one draught of this on earth wars would be fought and nations betrayed" (p. 42). Having drained one gourd, Ransom is about to pick another when he suddenly realizes that he is no longer hungry or thirsty. Although he is drawn by the desire to repeat a pleasure so intense, it seems better for him not to eat another at this time.

Shortly thereafter he has a similar experience when he finds a group of "bubble trees." These trees draw up water from the ocean, enrich it in some way, and produce spheres that swell until they burst and emit a delicious fragrance. Before Ransom has discovered the nature of these trees, he puts out his hand to touch one. Instantly (since he has popped it) he gets what seems like a shower with a delicious scent. Now, having discovered the secret, he thinks of new possibilities. He could plunge through the trees, breaking many of the spheres at once, and enjoy the experience "multiplied tenfold." But, as in the case of the fruit, something restrains him.

> He had always disliked the people who encored a favourite air in the opera—"That just spoils it" had been his comment. But this now appeared to him as a principle of far wider application and deeper moment. This itch to have things over again, as if life were a film that could be unrolled twice or even made to work backwards . . . was it possibly the root of all evil? No: of course the love of money was called that. But money itself— perhaps one valued it chiefly as a defence against chance, a security for being able to have things over again, a means of arresting the unrolling of the film. (P. 48)

Ransom has a similar experience when he finds some bushes that bear oval green berries. These are good to eat, though they do not give "the orgiastic and almost alarming pleasure of the gourds, but rather the specific pleasure of plain food" (p. 49). As he eats, Ransom finds that a few of the berries have a bright red center and are especially tasty. He is tempted to look only for those with the red center but is again strongly restrained from doing so.

---

13. Lewis, *Perelandra* (New York: Macmillan, 1965), p. 42. Subsequent references to this v ork will be made parenthetically in the text.

"Now on earth," thought Ransom, "they'd soon discover how to breed these redhearts, and they'd cost a great deal more than the others." Money, in fact, would provide the means of saying *encore* in a voice that could not be disobeyed. (P. 50)

This theme is made even clearer in what is perhaps the central image of *Perelandra*. The planet is for the most part a world of floating islands, but it also has a Fixed Land. Its first two inhabitants, the Lady and the King, are permitted to go onto the Fixed Land but not to live or sleep there. And that prohibition becomes the focal point for the tempter—the UnMan sent there to introduce evil into an innocent world. He calls the Lady's attention to the fact that people who live on a fixed land cannot be easily separated, as she and the King have been. They can control their own destinies to some extent and need not—here he borrows her own metaphor—think of themselves as constantly "thrown into the wave." He suggests that the command to live only on the floating islands "stands between you and all settled life, all command of your days" (p. 117). In the end, however, when the UnMan has been defeated, the Lady comes to see the significance of that command.

> The reason for not yet living on the Fixed Land is now so plain. How could I wish to live there except because it was Fixed? And why should I desire the Fixed except to make sure—to be able on one day to command where I should be the next and what should happen to me? It was to reject the wave—to draw my hands out of Maleldil's, to say to Him, "Not thus, but thus"—to put in our own power what times should roll toward us . . . as if you gathered fruits together to-day for tomorrow's eating instead of taking what came. That would have been cold love and feeble trust. And out of it how could we ever have climbed back into love and trust again? (P. 208)

That is the message of the story—our problem with possessions is a failure to trust.

The Bible also tells a story—a story of creation corrupted by sin, redeemed, and finally restored. To think of possessions within that story is to see how dangerous is our eagerness to fashion our own security, how intricate is a proper attitude toward the good things of our world. A life of trust always involves a double movement: affirmation and negation, enjoyment and renunciation of things.

This double movement is grounded first in the fact of creation itself. Although the things of our world are proper sources of delight, they always remain *created* things. As gifts of the Creator, they reflect his goodness and glory. This means that they do more than offer enjoyment; they convey a message. They call us out of ourselves, both

delighting the heart *and* drawing it beyond created things to the
Creator. The true source of enjoyment is not, finally, *in* the things we
possess; it comes *through* them. Renunciation—if not of the thing
possessed, at least of the desire to possess—cannot be separated
from enjoyment. That is what the Lady learned on Perelandra: a re-
ceptive enjoyment of Maleldil's gift involved renunciation of the
fruit she had originally intended to eat.

It is because a double movement is required that no single attitude toward possessions can be recommended as the Christian one.
Some renunciation must always be present, but renunciation alone
cannot be the way all Christians must approach the problem of possessions. Moreover, renunciation is never to be an end in itself. It is
part of a total movement intended to honor, esteem, and affirm the
good gifts of the Creator. Nevertheless, because the biblical narrative is a story not only of creation but also of sin, renunciation must
take on increased importance in the Christian life. We do not only receive our possessions with glad hearts; we grasp after them, want
more than we need, take things sometimes at the expense of others,
and seek our security in an abundance of possessions. Fallen creatures do that: they want to grasp and retain, to store up rather than
to receive daily, to turn from what is given to what is desired—and
for such creatures the movement of negation built into the dialectic
of creation must often be experienced as painful renunciation.

Since the central problem is the self who does not trust, the renunciation asked is not finally of things or possessions. It is *self*-
renunciation, a mortifying and killing of that greedy, grasping, fallen self. Thus, the addition of fallenness to the Christian story
necessarily adds a severe, somewhat ascetic note. Christians must
always look with some suspicion upon luxuries. If we have more
than we need, others may have less than they need. If we enjoy considerable luxury, it may be difficult for our hearts to make the other
half of the double movement—to renounce as well as enjoy. And the
more abstract the form of our luxuries, the more dangerous they
may be. Emil Brunner makes the point clearly.

> Money is the abstract form of material goods. This abstraction,
> like all abstraction, includes both great potentialities and great
> dangers. . . . Where money has become the main material good,
> quantity tends to prevail over quality. The desire for wealth be-
> comes infinite. I cannot imagine an infinite number of concrete
> material goods, but I can easily add an indefinite number of
> ciphers to any given figure.[14]

---

14. Brunner, *Christianity and Civilisation*, Part 2: *Specific Problems*
(London: Nisbet, 1949), pp. 87-88.

Having noted this, Brunner himself goes on to qualify it. Although money, as an abstract form of possessions, may give rise to limitless craving, it remains true that "within the Christian faith motive is more important than structure."[15] But perhaps having granted that structure also shapes spirit, we should be less sanguine. Is it possible, for example, that delight in our work has become more difficult in a world in which money (or, a still greater abstraction, credit) has become the chief material good? Desire is refocused—and encouraged to become infinite. Without such an infinite scope for desire, advertising would play a far less important role than it does in our economic life. And it is, I think, a common observation—not nearly as paradoxical as it may at first seem—that advertising, by discouraging renunciation, makes enjoyment of the goods we possess more difficult. An unfocused and infinite desire always wants something more.

If the movement from creation to *sinful* creation adds a severely ascetic note to the Christian story, it is still true that enjoyment is the final goal. To such enjoyment and delight, incarnation and redemption lead. And however much room there may be for abstinence and renunciation in our present pilgrim condition, Christians trust that we are made to enjoy the vision of God. Incarnation is the sign that earthly goods remain objects of delight even in a fallen world. Redemption is the promise that abstinence is not the final word. At the center of Christian piety is a man slowly dying by torture, and it is no surprise that this should be a faith of martyrs and ascetics. But the God whom Christians worship is one who goes the way of self-renunciation in order to redeem the creation. At his right hand, the psalmist says, are pleasures forevermore (16:11).

Christians can, therefore, adopt and recommend no single attitude toward possessions. When they attempt to understand their lives within the world of biblical narrative, they are caught up in the double movement of enjoyment and renunciation. Neither half of the movement, taken by itself, is the Christian way of life. *Trust* is the Christian way of life. In order to trust, renunciation is necessary, lest we immerse ourselves entirely in the things we possess, trying to grasp and keep what we need to be secure. In order to trust, enjoyment is necessary, lest renunciation become a principled rejection of the creation through which God draws our hearts to himself. Indeed, affirmation must, I think, have the final word. Principled renunciation is more dangerous than principled enjoyment because created goods are channels through which the divine glory strikes us, and those who love and delight in any good thing may yet learn

---

15. Brunner, *Christianity and Civilisation*, p. 93.

to love God. The heart may be drawn from image to Reality. But to renounce all enjoyment of created things—to delight in nothing— must *either* be only one part of a movement that, we trust, will end in enjoyment, *or* it must be hell.

The Story of an Encounter

David Heim

Can we see God's face in the movement of history? That seems a dauntingly large question with which to launch a conference on poverty. But as Max Stackhouse of Andover Newton Theological School made clear, the rise of Liberation Theology has pushed religious discussion to this level of theological reflection. The liberationists see God in the struggle of the poor to overturn the social and political conditions that oppress them. Gustavo Gutiérrez asserts that "the kingdom of God is expressed in the manifestation of his justice and love in favor" of the poor.

Are the liberationists right? Stackhouse answered No, or rather, Not entirely. And with varying degrees of emphasis and for varying reasons, some of them theological and others having more to do with social and political analysis, a great many of the other twenty-six participants were inclined to agree. Liberation thought was far from endorsed; yet it could not be evaded either, as the title of the conference indicates. By linking a particular theological understanding of the poor to a Marxist or quasi-Marxist analysis of how the needs of the poor should be met, liberation thought has forcefully joined the questions of what the Christian and Jewish understanding of the poor is and what social policy is most consistent with that understanding.

THE HISTORIZING IMPULSE

For Stackhouse, the most problematic and dangerous aspect of liberation thought is its tendency to historicize the meaning of the Christian gospel, identifying it exclusively with the struggle of the poor. To see the Holy Spirit at work in history dismantling unjust and oppressive structures is, Stackhouse recognized, an authentic element of the Protestant tradition, especially that part of the tradition traceable to the radical wing of the Reformation and sectarian reformers like Thomas Müntzer. Given this tradition, it is understandable that mainline Protestants have the "nagging suspicion" that the liberationists are right. In fact, in light of their "cool alliance" with the Enlightenment, mainline Protestants could stand to learn from the liberationists a more dynamic and concrete sense of the power of the Holy Spirit. But Stackhouse is equally certain that once one makes the move of "sacralizing" the poor—identifying the poor as the locus of the Holy Spirit—one loses the critical purchase necessary for evaluating their struggle. "All you have is go with the flow, go with the movement. And that makes it rough should the movement go in the direction of a Hitler."

The theological challenge, as Stackhouse sees it, is to integrate the insights of the "new Müntzerites" with other classical themes in Protestant thought. Unfolding a trinitarian motif implicit in his historical survey, he argued that the Müntzerite emphasis on the Holy Spirit—on the immanence of God in historical realities—needs to be joined both to a Calvinist emphasis on the sovereignty and transcendence of God and a Lutheran emphasis on individual redemption in Christ. "I am an unreconstructed trinitarian," Stackhouse reported. Along with affirming the revolutionary power of the Holy Spirit, he urged, "we have to work on the formation of individual character, the conversion of individuals in Jesus Christ, the transformation of individual identity, and we have to recover the notion of living under a sovereign creator God."

This formulation of the theological issues seemed on target to James Skillen of the Association for Public Justice. Speaking out of the Calvinist tradition, he observed that Calvinism, for all its emphasis on transforming the world according to God's purposes, has instilled a certain humility about how much humans can accomplish and how much the world can be transformed. "If Protestantism gives up an understanding of creation as having God's sovereign structure to it, a structure that we can't recreate or do away with, and if it gives up the recognition of the transcendence of the eschaton, then we really have reached the end of Protestantism," he said.

Brigitte Berger of Wellesley needed little persuading about the perils of historicist thinking. She recalled that the German philosopher Martin Heidegger, lacking the philosophic apparatus to resist the apparent movement of history, had been led to embrace Nazism, saying in effect, "this is the sweep of our time and we have to go with it." If that is what liberation thought brings us to, Berger said she wants no part of it.

Stackhouse noted that on that occasion Heidegger had been paraphrasing the last chapter of Hegel's *Philosophy of Right*—neatly illustrating the secular strand of historicist thought that, through Marx and others, has surfaced in Liberation Theology.

Cogent as this critique of historicism appeared, Dennis McCann, who teaches as DePaul, wondered if there really is a clear alternative. What philosophic ground did Stackhouse stand on that allowed him to critique historicism? Did he have access to truths that were not historically conditioned? Historicism is much more pervasive than Stackhouse was letting on, he suggested. "I can't imagine there isn't a single person here who wouldn't own up to being at least moderately historicist, if not radically and consistently so," he said. "So we can't look at the problem of the 'new Thomas Müntzer' as an us-versus-them question. Rather, we are on a continuum together, grappling with a common problem. Historicism means that we are all in some way trying to live out 'the heretical imperative.' The illusion of orthodoxy, in a nonhistoric sense, has been shattered, and therefore certain ways of relating to our traditions are no longer possible."

This problem is particularly pertinent to discussions of poverty, McCann said, since the biblical literature on the topic is diverse and ambiguous. There is bound to be an explosion of interpretations, all of them possessing some degree of plausibility, in an age when there is no authoritative institution or tradition that is believed to be outside the vagaries of history. Richard Neuhaus, director of the Rockford Institute Center on Religion and Society, asked McCann if he meant to deny the possibility of locating transcendent points of reference with respect to justice and order. McCann replied that he did hold out for such principles and was committed to public dialogue about them, but at the same time he recognized that the "epistemological warrants for the universal claims I make are very shaky."

In raising the epistemological question, McCann had put his finger on a problem Stackhouse had been wrestling with in his work in theological ethics. "Is it possible to identify, in dialogue or philosophically rooted theology, transcontextual and transhistorical principles?" Stackhouse thought it crucial to answer Yes. "If you don't have a notion that some things are right and wrong, true and just, outside the mere flux of things, then we really are lost in the 'fluxus quo.' We have no way of assessing what is going on; we can merely be within it. We end up with the deconstructionists, with Jacques Derrida and Richard Rorty, having dialogues for which there is no *logue*—no *logos*—and conversations in which there is no common ground for assessing what is being said."

Stackhouse said that he was not looking for orthodoxy "in the sense of creeds that you have to follow or you get clobbered," but orthodoxy in the sense of knowing that there are some "straight truths." Otherwise, the only orthodoxy we have is that of particular confessing groups at particular times in particular contexts.

MODERN MONTANISM

The epistemological basis for modern moral philosophy was not an issue many of the participants were prepared to pursue. Walter Block wanted to focus attention on the contemporary meaning of the "sacralizing" of the poor. He pointed out that when medieval Christianity had ascribed a sacred quality to poverty, it had in mind the poverty voluntarily embraced by monks and priests. Today, however, the poor who are being sacralized are poor not voluntarily but by coercion; they are the victims of the powers that be.

Neuhaus thought this an important distinction, and he suggested that the use of the term *victims* helps illuminate the contemporary sense that the poor are pitted against the rest of society, against whom they have a grievance. "The people who followed the heroic virtues of monasticism and poverty were presumably exemplars of a possibility that was there for everyone, and they were 'ahead' of others in terms of virtue," he said. "But in the sacralization of victims, the victims (or the revolutionary proletariat, whatever language one uses) are against the rest of us."

Speaking of the poor as victims implicitly acknowledges that their poverty could be avoided. The fact that we think this way, George Weigel, who directs the James Madison Foundation, pointed out, is a sign that we no longer live in the medieval cosmos—and hence that that older understanding of the sacredness of poverty must be reformulated. "We now have a situation in which poverty is not necessary. That's a kind of shattering challenge to a lot of Christian thought. How can you be affluent or even middle class but poor in spirit? How do we develop an ethic and spirituality of abundance rather than scarcity? These are the cutting-edge questions that aren't being addressed very forcefully, certainly not in North American Christianity. This leaves the field of argument to first-stage Liberation Theology."

Michael Novak of American Enterprise Institute pressed a similar point. "The whole context of this meeting is that we can do something about poverty. In the last two hundred years, for the first time in history, you can imagine a world without poverty." In Müntzer's day, "there was no way the poor were going to escape being poor. The only thing you could do was sacralize them, tell them they are Jesus Christ, make them feel better, and license them to destroy."

The tendency to take a "mystical" view of the poor as the liberationists do, Novak said, is part of a long-standing "gnostic temptation" in Christian and Jewish thought. Gnosticism—which lies behind the thought of Gutiérrez, Marx, and Müntzer—"gives up trying patiently to change the structures of the world and of the flesh and looks for some spiritual, instant redemption, some magical key. There is a deep tendency in the West, on both the wild right and the wild left, to look for this magical key."

Novak was clear about what had created the historical watershed: the rise of capitalism. If one takes a decidedly unmystical view of the poor, and considers those mundane institutions that have generated wealth in the modern era—such things as savings and loans and private corporations—one can figure out the ways by which poor people become nonpoor. Umberto Eco's popular novel *The Name of the Rose* is a "parable of our time" in this regard, Novak mused. "The dialectic of *The Name of the Rose* is between an Englishman and a set of monks who have a mystical view of the poor. This is the North-South dialogue. And in the parable, the way out is something very humble: using your eyes and hands to see what actually works."

ASSESSING LIBERATION THEOLOGY

These reflections prompted Neuhaus to suggest that if, as Stackhouse had argued, Liberation Theology signified the "return of Müntzer," then this return was radically out of sync with the world. To take an older vision of the poor, derived from a static world, and make it the vehicle for social change represented a "radical chronological confusion."

Lawrence Mead is a social scientist at NYU much engaged in current debates on welfare policy, and he reported that he, too, is disturbed by the way liberation thought places responsibility for poverty on external structures. Liberation theologians say that "the poor are not responsible, society is responsible"—an approach Mead considers permissive and ultimately counterproductive. His own research into the dynamics of poverty indicates that the poor are not so much the victims of oppressive structures as they are in need of stable structures that require a degree of individual responsibility.

"On the whole," said Mead, "poverty in the U.S. or the Third World is due to disorder—to the lack not only of justice in the macro-economic sense but more fundamentally the lack of the rule of law, of equal opportunity, of any trustworthy public realm. Those structures depend on there being an impartial rule of law for which everyone accepts responsibility. That is missing in the Third World and in inner cities of the U.S. It isn't going to help today's poor merely to say that the rest of society should give them what they want. What they want on the whole is immediate sustenance and immediate benefits, whereas what they need is the rule of law. That isn't an element of Liberation Theology that I hear very loudly."

As an active churchman, Mead is aware of how liberation thought has permeated the churches. He suggested that its effect there has been to set rich against poor in a way that is not only unproductive but personally painful. "In Liberation Theology, the poor have authority over the rest of us. They get to judge us. That means very concretely in the church that poor people get to make the demands and better-off people have to meet them. I've found in the churches to which I've belonged it is almost impossible for me to get my agenda on the table. Poor people get the attention, and I'm supposed to take care of them. If you are an educated WASP man, you are responsible for all the world's problems. There is no good news for you. In fact, I find religious moralists persuaded by liberationist perspectives to be the most judgmental people I have ever encountered."

Stackhouse suggested that Mead was misreading the judgmental aspect of Liberation Theology. "The poor *do* judge us," he said. "Just go spend some time among them. But that is not what the Liberation Theology movement is about. Theologically speaking, we are judged because *there are* poor. And we are judged by more ultimate powers than the poor represent. And insofar as we remain inactive in the face of poverty, there is a deeper and longer-range kind of judgment on our heads. That is the weight Protestantism properly feels and is trying, fumblingly, to come to grips with."

Stackhouse agreed, however, that there is something permissive about the liberationists' focus on liberation and not law, Exodus and not Mt. Sinai. "The liberationists have made a partially correct choice when they talk about liberation using the metaphor of the exodus—coming out from the oppressive structures of pharaoh. What I have unsuccessfully searched for is any fundamental treatment of coming to the holy mountain at which the law of God is established and a covenant is made—the covenant being an eternal and unchangeable law."

This extended and concerted attack on liberation thought struck Ken Jameson and Paul Sigmund as exaggerated and to some extent unwarranted. Jameson, who teaches economics at Notre Dame, had spent some time in base communities in Mexico and Peru, and his experience there had not led him to worry about their permissiveness. "If there is one outstanding characteristic of the base communities, it is that they inculcate responsibility. They call people to take responsibility for their lives, for reading the Bible, for coming to meetings, for dealing with problems such as stray dogs and getting water. To me, one of the most impressive things was seeing the sense of responsibility people take on when they get involved with the option for the poor."

Part of our problem may be that we too quickly interpret Liberation Theology in terms of what it means in North America, Jameson suggested. "One of our problems with the poor is their profligate habits. But the base communities come down very hard on that. They require people to work hard. They have an ethic of work rather than an ethic of 'Let's take something that someone gives us.' There is a real sense, too, of finding God in a very particular fashion in this experience. I don't think we should lose sight of this and say that Liberation Theology is simply revolution. The base communities' interest in popular religiosity, and learning from it, is very important."

Neuhaus could well imagine that there is a gap between theory and practice in the base communities. The "Marxist mentors" may be producing "Calvinist graduates"—people who have learned self-control and respect for legitimate authority. "There is an enormous gap between how the Juan Luis Segundos and the Gustavo Gutiérrezes interpret the base communities and their reality."

Sigmund, who teaches politics at Princeton and directs that school's Latin American Studies Program, thought the discussion was overstating the Marxist dimension of liberation thought. The movement did propose a quasi-Marxist structuralist critique of capitalism, especially in the beginning, but this element has become increasingly less prominent, partly as a result of the critique of the movement in Latin America and at the Vatican. The other side of the movement, which was there from the beginning, Sigmund argued, was a more populist strain, which emphasized participation, empowerment, involvement. The populist element in the base communities made it difficult to generalize about them. "Populism can be radical, but it can also be reactionary. The base communities can tell you a lot of different things; they don't necessarily promote a structuralist anticapitalism as the solution to all their problems." As for the theorists of the movement, they display considerable diversity as well. If one is going to cite Segundo or Gutiérrez, one must identify which Segundo or Gutiérrez—that of 1968 or 1986. Sigmund stated that in Gutiérrez's most recent book there is no Marx at all.

LIBERATING COMMUNITIES, RESPONSIBLE INDIVIDUALS

Mead expressed some doubt that the base communities are actually able to inculcate the sense of personal responsibility that is integral to the Protestant tradition. To say that "the community" takes responsibility is too abstract, he said. "The minute you say 'the group' is responsible, responsibility gravitates to the strong against the weak." But Sigmund felt Mead was exaggerating the dangers of communitarianism. It's hard to evade responsibility when you are part of a group of eight meeting every week, he said. Gilbert Meilaender wondered if Mead was not pressing his concern for individual responsibility too far. "The Protestant emphasis is not simply on individual responsibility. Individuals are never separate from the community that sustains them. You can tout individual responsibility all you want, but don't affix the adjective *Protestant* to it."

Picking up on the theme of individualism and community, Novak commented that an ecumenical crossover seemed to be taking place in recent years: Protestants were embracing Jewish-Catholic themes of community while Catholics were gaining new respect for individualism. But to Novak's mind, the Catholics weren't moving fast enough in this direction. He saw too much reliance on the rhetoric of "solidarity," a term that in his view denies individualism and indeed the importance of regarding individuals as distinct entities. "It's an extremely dangerous notion—dangerous, for example, for dissent," he said. "Catholics have a lot more they need to say about the individual, and in places like Latin America it's very damaging that they don't."

As for the base communities themselves, however, Stackhouse suggested that they are not really communities in the classic sense but a new form of associationalism—intentionally formed groups fostering new modes of discipline.

The notion that Liberation Theology is better in practice than in theory struck Dennis McCann as a Niebuhrian irony. Perhaps liberation thought is most problematic in American colleges and seminaries, he said, where intellectuals can theorize about the poor without coming into contact with them. Such contact tends to disabuse one of the idea that the poor have qualitatively different insights into social problems than the rest of us.

"My theoretical resistance to the hermeneutical privilege of the oppressed, or the sacralization of poverty, stems from my experience in the sixties; the poor people with whom I worked would not let me make that move," said McCann. "They were not about to be put on a pedestal to solve whitey's problems of a religious and spiritual nature. And they were contemptuous of limousine liberals who came into the ghetto looking for that kind of transfer of authority. We were privileged to be immunized against that behavior because we all lived together. Any form of patronization—and sacralizing the poor is a form of patronization—is counterproductive not only for the poor but for whitey. It raises the question of what whitey is doing among the poor anyway. Is he working out his own salvation or is he part of the solution?"

One of the virtues of the U.S. Catholic bishops' pastoral letter on the economy, *Economic Justice for All*, is that it does not indulge in that sort of posturing, said McCann. Rather than pit one class against the other or call on the nonpoor to negate who they are and the resources they have "through some completely irrelevant guilt trip," the bishops issued a universal call to build a just society.

Peter Steinfels, a former editor of *Commonweal* now with the *New York Times*, did not want to see the hermeneutic of the poor abandoned entirely, however. Though he feels that a "positivistic hermeneutic" of the poor ought to be rejected, he said he thought the bishops were challenging Christians, and the church as a whole, to consider where they stand in relation to the poor and how this position affects their perspective. "Should the church, as an institution, be sitting in certain places? Should it have invested its money in certain ways and put people in certain positions?" These questions have obvious relevance in Latin America, where the church is, in some places, very much a middle-class or upper-middle-class operation.

McCann urged that the bishops' position might best be characterized as a "hermeneutic of solidarity" rather than an endorsement of a "hermeneutical privilege." Admitting that "solidarity" is a problematic term for the reasons Novak outlined, he still finds it useful. "I suspect what *solidarity* means is not that you abdicate responsibility for your own development or that you try to become something that you're not. Rather, it refers to a process of empathy and imagination, of learning how other people think through genuine interaction. Besides speaking on behalf of the oppressed and defending the defenseless, solidarity means seeing things from the point of view of the poor and the powerless, and assessing lifestyles and politics and social institutions from the side of the poor. There is a call to conversion here, a call to go to a different place."

WHO ARE THE POOR?

If the poor are not uniquely the bearers of the Holy Spirit, then who are they? And what makes them poor? Glenn Loury, an economist at Harvard's John F. Kennedy School of Government, thought it was time to begin making some empirical distinctions.

"Poverty in Latin America, among rural peasants who own no land and are subject to the oppressive influence of an oligarchy that controls the state apparatus and the economy, strikes me as a profoundly different phenomenon than poverty in the United States," said Loury. "And a preferential option for the poor—the locating of a special theological significance in the experience and fact of poverty—strikes me as meaning something different in the one context from what it means in the other. It makes a lot of sense to say that people are dispossessed when they are deprived of the ability to own land and to better their lives through direct, commonsense actions. It's another thing entirely in a nation of immigrants, where among those whom we count as poor are people we can be pretty sure are not going to be poor ten years from now. Even in the U.S., who are we talking about as 'the poor'? There is a lot of in and out: a lot of people are poor today who are not poor tomorrow. For example, there is a difference between a household headed by a woman with little education who bore her children early and a household where the main breadwinner has been unemployed but expects that circumstance to change shortly."

Neuhaus commented that religious leaders have a tendency to ignore these kinds of distinctions and to speak in a sweeping way about "the poor" without concerning themselves with "actual people and their circumstances and why they are churning in and out of this community we call 'the poor.'" This failure "to disaggregate the poor is a failure to take people seriously."

One way to take poor people seriously is to stop thinking of them as different from the rest of us, said Loury. "I chafe at the we-they distinction implicit in our discussion of the poor. We presuppose that the poor are incapable of doing things themselves. I worry that there is something contemptuous about a compassion that denies its objects the possibility we assume is within our own grasp. Everyone around this table has free will; we are more or less in control of our destiny. But 'they,' it seems, have been dehumanized and are without that capacity. 'They' can cut each other on Saturday night, and what can we do but say, 'Well, we couldn't expect anything else from them: they're ghetto people.' Their moral life can decay, and all we can do is wring our hands about how they have been victimized by our social order."

Loury had struck a theme very near to Lawrence Mead's heart: one helps the poor not by treating them as people who need help but as people from whom something can be expected. His complaint about the Catholic bishops' letter is that when it comes to promoting policy options, it advances a largely welfarist approach which assumes that the poor are passive recipients. "That view of the poor as helpless, as not responsible, is in fact the problem," he contended. So long as government merely offers benefits to the poor, it won't be able to help them overcome the behavioral "dysfunctions" that keep them impoverished.

"One cause of long-term poverty is the problem the poor have in coping, in dealing with daily challenges such as work," said Mead. "It isn't true that jobs aren't available. There are jobs, but for some reasons that we don't totally understand, this group has difficulty sticking to employment. The salience of this kind of problem has led secular policymakers to wrestle with what it means to help the poor. We've started to say that it isn't adequate to provide certain benefits, that we also have to do something about the coping problem. But this wrestling is completely absent from the bishops' letter and from any other discussions of which I'm aware among churchpeople. Why is there no wrestling among the churches with the implications of dysfunctions for the meaning of charity and justice?"

Loury thought the bishops' reticence on this issue could be understood politically. After all, the bishops didn't operate in a vacuum. "In the age of Reagan, of the retrenchment of social programs and redefinition of social obligations, putting weight on personal responsibility might be seen as lending support to the retrogressive side of the public policy debate." But that would be the wrong interpretation, Loury thought; indeed, the best chance for formulating an effective public policy for the poor is to confront head-on the patterns of irresponsibility among the poor. "If we lie to ourselves about what is going on in the ghetto, if we create myths, then we may be building up the kind of resentment and contempt that will ultimately fuel reaction. Maybe the lying we did to ourselves about the ghetto in the 1960s and seventies is partly responsible for the reaction we are reaping now, particularly among the working-class ethnics who formed such a significant part of the Democratic coalition. Telling the truth—which I associate with holding people accountable for the consequences of behaviors that are abjectly wrong, immoral, and dysfunctional—may contribute to an environment in which people, honestly confronting their mutual obligation, can come to some understandings about public policy that are more secure in the long run than what we build upon fabrications."

Mary Jo Bane, who also teaches at the Kennedy School of

Government, agreed that there are dysfunctional behaviors among the poor. "If you get pregnant at sixteen, or you get a girl pregnant at sixteen, you are likely to be poor." But this was only part of the story. "There are reasons why girls get pregnant that are not just tied to original sin—reasons that have to do with the kind of economic opportunities in their communities." This being the case, she said, we ought to be paying more attention to whether we, as a society, are making sure that if people do behave well they can in fact better their lives.

THE POOR AND THE BUDGET

Allison Stokes wanted to discuss this question in terms of national priorities. It struck her as significant that the Catholic bishops' letter on the economy had followed their letter on peace and nuclear weapons. To Stokes, a chaplain at Yale, this juxtaposition called attention to the fact that as a nation we have chosen to spend a great deal of money on instruments of death—money that could be spent on behalf of the poor.

Larry Mamiya, who teaches religion at Vassar, also thought defense spending deserved some scrutiny at this conference. He recalled that when President Eisenhower had warned in the late 1950s about the development of a massive military-industrial complex, he had said that "every bomber built, every missile made, every ship launched, is in some ultimate sense a theft from those who hunger and those who need shelter." Mamiya asserted that the current investment in the Strategic Defense Initiative, or Star Wars, expected to run to $1 trillion over several years, is particularly dubious given the many questions about its strategic effectiveness and contribution to peace. That $1 trillion could be spent for alleviating poverty. Mamiya noted that he has listened to many complaints about the ineffectiveness of government spending on the poor and how it has caused the poor to be irresponsible—but what about the ineffectiveness of defense spending, he wanted to know, and what about the irresponsibility of defense contractors? "We have been criticizing the culture of dependency that federal government programs have created among the poor. We also need to look at the culture of dependency developed in the military-industrial complex."

Jameson was reminded by this discussion of an editorial he had seen in the *Wall Street Journal* endorsing SDI not only for defense reasons but for the sake of all those Ph.D. scientists whose careers are based on SDI research. The consensus seemed to be that we find the same kind of dependency and irresponsibility on the part of the rich as we find among the poor—behavior that in both cases undermines the social compact.

Novak characterized Stokes's dramatic contrast between money spent on nuclear weapons and money spent on the poor as a "cheap issue." He argued that "Not much money goes into nuclear weapons. It's about one-ninth of the defense budget, and the defense budget isn't as large as the social welfare budget by a long shot. And insofar as the Catholic bishops are against nuclear weapons, as they say they are, and are urging a stronger reliance on conventional forces, they are calling for a lot more money to be spent on defense than anybody has contemplated. I think the bishops have taken a cheap shot in attacking nuclear weapons, which they can't really intend. If they do, they haven't thought through the consequences of it—above all the consequences for the national budget."

The discussion appeared to be headed into a consideration of the pros and cons of defense spending—a topic many participants thought was too far afield.

"How can we have this discussion," Loury wondered, "without assaying the intention of the Soviet Union, the appropriate role of America in the world, and the tactical and strategic situations in the Middle East and Central Europe? This is all in the abstract."

Mead stated that poverty and defense spending are two separate issues. "It isn't reasonable to say, 'Ah, the poor are needy, therefore we should cut defense.' What you should say is, 'The poor are needy. What do we need for a social policy?'" Whether a trade-off is necessary between the two kinds of spending will become clear only when one has decided what social policy is needed.

Neuhaus suggested that this discussion was helping to clarify an essential point: "Even if there were another $1 trillion available for social programs, that would not solve our problem. Our problem is that the programs themselves, no matter how much money we put into them, are not doing what we think ought to be done with respect to helping the poor, and in fact may be exacerbating the situation."

But there was by no means a consensus on this point. The relevant issue, Peter Steinfels observed again, was which poor we are talking about. More money could help a lot of the poor, though not some others, and there might be others whom more government spending might actually harm. "There are people in short-term poverty whom we could probably keep from going into a spiral of problems if our procedures were better and we had more money."

Bane, who had spent the last three years running New York State's welfare department, was also sure that some government programs were succeeding and that more funding, in certain areas, anyway, would be a good investment. "Spending on the poor has had dramatic results among the elderly and disabled—which is where the huge growth in welfare spending has taken place over the last twenty years," she noted. "The poverty rate among the elderly is now below the poverty rate of the population as a whole—and I think that's related to spending. I think we could do a lot more along the lines of Social Security for the disabled and others unable to work. There are other areas where we need to make investments—in Head Start, which still serves only a small proportion of the population and which has been demonstrated to be effective, and in employment and training programs. The most controversial area is welfare benefits per se. In New York State the total package of benefits comes to about the poverty line—so this is not a get-rich-quick scheme. And the low level of welfare benefits has something to do with the fact that thirty thousand people are being sheltered in welfare hotels and city shelters."

The programs that Bane was touting were anathema to Walter Block. It is just such government interventions in the economy that, in his view, skew the market, create unemployment, and limit opportunities. To look to government to solve problems of poverty or unemployment is like inviting the fox in to guard the chicken coop, he said. He maintained that such things as welfare, unions, the minimum wage, tariffs, and rent control constitute the "active oppression of the poor." Given this limited view of the state, Block took special exception to the Catholic bishops' declaration that "all people have a right to life, food, clothing, shelter, rest, medical care, education, and employment" on the grounds that it takes the concept of rights far beyond its usual meaning in the American political tradition. He views true rights as negative rights—that is, the right we have to be free from certain kinds of interference and coercion. To introduce positive economic rights, such as rights to food, clothing, and shelter, is to confuse rights and wealth, he argued; besides suggesting an enormous new role for government in guaranteeing these rights, this approach disrupts ordinary ways of thinking about charity and morality and is philosophically confusing. "Under the bishops' view, there can be no such thing as charity, for anything a rich person gives to a poor person is already that poor person's due—the poor having a 'right' against the rich." Economic rights also have the odd effect of making acts of God immoral, said Block: a storm or earthquake can violate people's rights to shelter and food—"yet in ordinary language we would hardly call that a violation of anyone's rights."

IN DEFENSE OF THE WELFARE STATE

Throughout the conference, Block warned against relying on government action to solve social problems, and he emphasized that it has been the initiative of free individuals operating in a free market that has generated wealth and raised the standard of living. There was considerable sympathy at the conference for the idea that the positive role of government has been much exaggerated in recent years and that large-scale government action is unlikely to alleviate the woes of the poor. But none of the other participants embraced the highly limited view of the state that Block articulated. Robert Benne of Roanoke College, for example, argued vigorously for a greater reliance on the private sector and on decentralized approaches in combatting poverty, but in light of Block's remarks he felt constrained to add that the welfare system on the whole is a positive force and that it needs to be improved rather than jettisoned. Libertarians such as Block, he suggested, operate with a "thin" notion of justice and a much more limited sense of human obligation than is found in Christian tradition.

Glenn Loury is well known as a critic of relying on government assistance to generate economic development. However, Block's remarks prompted him to defend the legitimacy of certain kinds of government intervention. Reflecting on the meaning of slavery for blacks in America, he said that there seemed to be something "ahistorical" about Block's resistance to tinkering with the marketplace. "I think you all know that I am not making one of those simpleminded arguments: 'Slavery was horrible, therefore let's do the following . . .' I want to observe that slavery is a historical and political fact that operates continually in our life. I don't know that we get a wiser public policy by pretending that it didn't occur. If we do take it into account, we are likely to conclude that Bedford-Stuyvesant, Harlem, the east side of Detroit, and the like are unacceptable as permanent phenomena of our public life and that we are required to act. Those actions might include limiting our right to property. They might even mean that the state will take race into account when it undertakes some of its enterprises. We can argue about the extent to which it should be taken into account, but at the very least those historical facts push up against pristine libertarian principles."

Loury went on to say that he did share Block's misgivings about economic rights, however, and he pointed out that the Catholic bishops' way of addressing the question is highly ambiguous. "There is a difference between a right to work that means a union cannot prevent you from working and a right to work that means the state will employ you if no one else will," he noted.

But Peter Steinfels did not think these distinctions should divert attention from the moral concern that had led the bishops to invoke the term *rights*. That concern might be grasped by considering the way in which education is a right of sorts in the United States, he suggested. "Legally we don't have the right to an education; we only have the right to an *equal* education. Nonetheless, we do have a moral right to an education. To my knowledge there isn't a school board in the country that has made the decision to close its schools. If they did, we would soon see that we have a constitutional, legal right to an education. By that I mean to say that the moral right would be translated into law. I think the bishops are saying that we ought seriously to consider putting energy and attention into some kind of parallel development in terms of economic rights."

Novak, who was also uneasy with the language of economic rights, thought Steinfels's example was a good one, especially since it demonstrated that there are ways of providing certain goods without using the language of rights. The bishops were unclear about whether they meant individual rights or social goals, and to Novak's mind it is much preferable to use the language of goals.

THE MEDIATING STRUCTURES

Observing that the discussion had been emphasizing both personal and governmental responsibility, sociologist Robert Hill expressed the hope that this meant the conferees could get beyond the simplistic dichotomy of either blaming the victim or blaming the system. He suggested that one way to avoid that dichotomy is to focus on the role of "mediating structures"—a term that was advanced a decade ago by Neuhaus and Peter Berger to describe such institutions as the neighborhood, the family, and the church, which mediate between individual lives and the large, impersonal structures of society, such as the welfare system. "The thing that is so helpful about the mediating structures concept is that it says most of the factors responsible for upward mobility are nongovernmental," said Hill. Instead of looking to government, we can look to the effectiveness and responsiveness of mediating structures, he suggested, and instead of looking only to individual initiative, we can encourage the mediating structures that are closest to individual life. The strength of mediating structures was evident to Hill in the capacity black families have shown to care for children needing foster homes. He noted that there are one million black children in the United States being cared for informally by relatives. At the same time, there are one hundred thousand black children in foster-care institutions waiting to be placed in a home. How is it, Hill wondered, that the informal kinship mechanism, the mediating structure, can find places for one million but the government can't find places for one-tenth that many? The answer, it seems, is that government is simply not an effective institution for providing foster care; it seems better equipped to keep children in limbo. "I want to blame the system here," he said. The mediating structures approach reveals what can be accomplished by focusing on people's capacities, not their deficiencies. "We look at the one daughter in a family that has a child out of wedlock and we ask what the family did wrong. Why don't we look at the other three sisters who didn't have their kids out of wedlock and ask what they did right? We should not equate the poor with incapacity or a lack of resources. There are segments of the poor that have capacities and can be very significant levers for upward mobility."

Robert Woodson, president of the National Center for Neighborhood Enterprise, warmly affirmed Hill's remarks and was anxious to point out some financial considerations that explain why government-funded agencies are so often ineffective. Government money is allocated to foster-care agencies, he said, on the basis of the number of children being cared for. This means that these institutions have little incentive to see that children are permanently placed in homes. This dynamic surfaces in church-sponsored agencies as well, insofar as they too are dependent on government funds—and hence wind up being "church in name only."

Woodson extended his analysis to the welfare system as a whole, which over the past two decades has put more and more money into the delivery of services to the poor rather than direct transfers of money. By treating people as clients or consumers of services rather than as people responsible for themselves, those who are providing the services tend to perpetuate conditions of dependency. Indeed, since their own livelihood depends on there being people who need their services, those in the helping professions have a "perverse incentive for maintaining a group of people incapacitated." Woodson cited a recent study of welfare spending in New York State made by the Community Services Society which found that $14.8 billion in federal, state, and private funds were spent in one year on the 1.2 million poor people in the state. Where did all that money go? According to the CSS, 74 cents of every dollar went to those providing services, not to the poor people themselves. Woodson considers this damning evidence that the welfare system is benefitting the wrong people.

Bane found this analysis highly misleading. Yes, New York State does spend about fifteen or sixteen billion dollars on programs for the poor. But slightly over half of that amount goes to Medicaid. Some Medicaid money gets paid to doctors—to service providers. "But you should also know that slightly over half of that Medicaid money goes for the expenses of old people in nursing homes. I find it hard to put that kind of spending in the category of 'spending on services that makes the poor irresponsible.'"

Loury stated that a good many of those old people in nursing homes have children with substantial economic assets. Does that make sense, he wanted to know, in light of the fact that Medicaid dollars are ostensibly earmarked for the poor?

Bane wanted to pursue the idea presented by Woodson and Hill that private agencies such as the church could be more effective than the state in the area of foster care. She saw some formidable difficulties with this approach. To begin with, children come into foster care because state authorities have decided that they are being abused or neglected. Taking custody of children from parents is a state function, Bane noted. "Do the churches really want to do that? And do churches or voluntary organizations feel they can play the role of watching out for abused children?" A further problem arises once children are in the care of an institution: are the children being treated equally in the various institutions? This question has arisen lately in New York because the Catholic Church is questioning whether it should take non-Catholics into its foster-care institutions. And if it does, is it required to provide adolescents with family planning services—in violation of church teaching? "The rule, in terms of fairness, has been Yes—that this is not a religious issue. The difficulty comes when there are more non-Catholics coming into care than non-Catholic agencies. Do we really want to allow the Catholics, who have a lot of beds and very admirable institutions, to be able to say, 'No, we just want Catholics, and if we do take non-Catholics we are going to require that they behave like Catholics in our institutions'?"

Neuhaus thought this quite a reasonable thing for the Catholics to say: "We will take fewer children, but we will do it our way." Such a decision need not necessarily mean that the Catholics would exclude non-Catholics from their institutions; it need mean only that the homes would be run according to Catholic principles.

Bane, thinking of the state's position in all of this, still saw a difficulty: "Would I have the right, as a state agency, to place a Jewish child in that kind of situation?" However much we might like voluntary agencies to attend to functions such as foster care, she concluded, "there are genuine gaps and issues of fair treatment that make it too simple to say—even in this area where the churches have a clear mandate to care for children—that it can be easily done."

The debate over foster care made it clear to Loury that there was a pressing need for the conferees to distinguish the various spheres of public and private life and to identify the sphere in which certain kinds of judgments and services are most appropriately rendered. Since the state has a monopoly on coercion, it makes sense that the act of taking a child away from a parent should be the responsibility of the state and be protected by requirements of due process. But judgments about sexual activity seem to belong to a different sphere. "Say I want to do something about a fifteen-year-old kid who's having sex. Who has the standing, and how do you get it, to say to another person, 'You should live your life this way'? That kind of judgment may be located outside the public sphere for a lot of reasons, some of them straightforward reasons of efficiency having to do with the location of information and with how discriminations are made."

Behind Loury's remarks was a question about what makes people change their behavior—and a suspicion that certain kinds of behavior can be influenced only at a personal level. Woodson developed a similar opinion after observing how youth gangs in Philadelphia had been led to stop fighting and to assume a responsible role in the community. "What was it that made a difference? The leaders in those neighborhoods could not offer better jobs, education, or housing—because they didn't have any of those things. What they had was spiritual leadership. They entered into a covenant with the young people."

Charles Murray, author of *Losing Ground*, had also been pondering what it is that enables some people to overcome social and economic hardships, and he had decided that, as a general rule, the more local and private the relationship between a person in need and the person giving the assistance, the more likely it is that the person in need will take responsibility for improving his situation.

Bane was not convinced by this line of argument, however. She pointed out that studies of nineteenth-century charitable endeavors indicated that it was precisely the personal nature of the helping relationships—"I'm helping you because I expect something from you"—that fostered exploitation. There is something to be said for keeping helping relationships public and impersonal.

THEOLOGY AND POLICY

The recurrent emphasis on efficiency and on the usefulness of mediating structures provoked James Skillen to raise a large question about method. Pointing directly to Robert Benne's contention that efficiency and decentralization (along with justice) are principles by which love can be translated into the public realm, Skillen wondered if there was anything specifically Christian about this approach. It seems to have more the flavor of "utilitarian pragmatism," he said. "We tend as Christians to start with a principle, such as love, and then go to problems, such as poverty, and ask how we can do the greatest good for the greatest number." A Christian social philosophy ought to offer something more than this, he argued, especially with regard to an understanding of the various institutions that play a role in helping the poor. Equipped with the knowledge that human beings are made in God's image and that institutions are the locus for the development of creaturely capabilities, Christians should have some insight into the nature of these institutions, what they should be doing, and what their specific responsibilities are. And yet the way Christians are employing the concept of mediating structures gives evidence of a pervasive utilitarianism, said Skillen. "Families, churches, and schools are not first of all mediating structures—as if the reason they exist is to mediate between individuals and the state. A family simply cannot be used by public policymakers to achieve all kinds of policy ends. This is one of the problems we have with schools: as various problems arise, we ask the schools to do all kinds of things that maybe they aren't designed to do. So the first problem for Christians is not public policy but the Christian meaning of church, family, school, and enterprise."

The notion that the primary social responsibility of Christians is not to formulate effective public policy had also occurred to Charles Murray. He threw out the question of whether Christians are called upon to do good at one remove. Specifically, he was curious about the relative worth of two types of Christian activists. "One devotes himself to working in soup kitchens and with local drug addicts, devoting a great deal of his personal attention and time to dealing with other human beings and their problems. The other doesn't do any of that, but devotes his time to lobbying in Washington to create government programs that help these same people. Where do these two people fall in the scheme of virtue? And how is this question affected by the effectiveness or ineffectiveness of what they are doing? Do they get credit for trying? Do they get credit for not having hubris about what they are doing—if they are not certain what the effects of their actions are going to be?"

Inasmuch as the room was full of policy-minded people, the unstated answer appeared to be Yes, that Christians are called to do good at one remove and that they are also called to be effective. Steinfels thought it was a mistake to see the alternatives as an either/or. In his experience, the more politically conscious Christians were, the more they were also involved in working personally with those in need.

Oberlin's Gilbert Meilaender tackled the question by saying that "Christians are called to different kinds of service." Rather than ranking the two approaches in a "scheme of virtue," he would embrace both in a "cosmos of callings." But he did think Murray had located a real point of tension in the Christian life between firsthand and secondhand expressions of love. One could see this tension in the struggle to decide how to respond to the needy people that show up at the church door. Many churches have consciously decided in recent years that rather than help such people directly, they will refer them to an appropriate agency, which can make sure they haven't just visited five other churches. However rational this decision may be, it seems unsatisfactory. "There is something about this approach that doesn't seem to capture what love is—love as the spontaneous, direct helping of the person who shows up at the door, without paying too much heed to whether on some occasion one might be taken advantage of."

PIETY AND POVERTY

To this point the conference had been preoccupied with a decidedly activist set of concerns: What do we do to help the poor, and what does it mean to help the poor? Periodically, Meilaender had registered, only partly in jest, his "despair" at the proceedings. He was, he allowed, a "quietest, abidingly pessimistic about whether anything can really be made better." In short, he joked, he was a "true Lutheran—not like Neuhaus."

As the discussion turned to his paper, it became clear that Meilaender's pessimism did not derive solely from the difficulty of locating the public policy correlatives of a concern for the poor. His fundamental problem was that by focusing on the need to do something about the poor, the discussion had attributed a significance to material things that the Christian tradition does not entirely endorse. "We need to permit and even nurture the ambiguity between poverty in the sense of lacking things and the poverty that is an inner spirit, and which might go along with considerable abundance," he said. "If we don't, there are some things that the theological tradition wants to say that we just won't be able to say, and we will fall into one sort of danger or another. Deep in this tradition is the sense that the inner spirit, however much it is shaped by external structures and things and possessions, is not finally determined by them."

Meilaender was well aware that this theology of inner detachment can be misused to justify complacency. "There are lots of people who would be very pleased to hear that it is simply a poverty of spirit that is asked of them," he granted. Nevertheless, this part of the Christian message cannot be abandoned.

Allison Stokes was worried that the need to detach oneself from possessions was peculiar to those who have many possessions. She recalled how black theologians such as James Cone had criticized mainstream theology for articulating the viewpoint of white middle-class Christians while ignoring the experience of blacks. Perhaps Meilaender's spirituality of possessions was equally ethnocentric. "If we think of the poor as those dying of hunger, the problem of possessions is not their problem; it's our problem."

Meilaender did not think it was fair, however, to label his position "purely North American." He thought of himself, anyway, as articulating a broadly Christian perspective. As for Stokes's example of the desperately hungry person, even here there is a spiritual dimension to the material circumstance: "Who knows to what great moral and spiritual evil such a person might be tempted by his desperate and hungry position? Having and not having always involve a spiritual and moral condition. It is a fundamental religious issue that has to be worked through. I'm not just focusing on people like us and what sort of guilt problems we might have."

Reflecting on his years as a pastor in a poor section of Brooklyn, Neuhaus said that he had found preaching on the dangers of riches to be meaningful to the poor precisely because it addressed them as spiritual beings. And as it happened, those who absorbed this message tended to succeed in practical terms, too. "The people who gave most generously and sacrificially were the people who generally did well, because they were the people who built relationships and who had a sense of living lives of ultimate consequence." Insofar as churches in the inner city today focus on the material deprivations of poverty and downplay the classic Christian concern for detachment from material conditions, they are downplaying one of the greatest contributions the church can make.

Murray thought this discussion quite pertinent to contemporary thinking about social policy, which is beginning to recognize the need to address issues of character formation. "We have rightly said that you cannot in any meaningful sense pursue happiness if you are starving, and so providing basic subsistence has been taken as the primary function of social policy toward the poor. But there are other things exceedingly important that you have to have if you are going to become a fulfilled human being. Take the whole issue of self-respect. If you take seriously the notion that self-respect is important and then attempt to understand how self-respect is acquired, and if you think about social policy with that issue as keenly in mind as material needs, then you might end up with a social policy that provides less in a material sense than you would otherwise."

Others were less sure of how to move from Meilaender's perspective back to social policy questions. There was, as Meilaender freely admitted, an individualizing aspect to his approach. Is the negotiation of one's relation to material things simply intuitive and subjective, Robert Benne wondered, or are there some rules of thumb that communities could use to hold individuals accountable?

ON POSSESSIONS

James Skillen thought that the dialectic of renunciation and enjoyment Meilaender had spelled out needed to be translated into communal terms, and he had some suggestions for how it might be done. "You make the very good point that one can easily develop a sort of prideful selfishness in deciding to live in reduced means—a decision that isn't really related to selflessness at all. Couldn't that point be made at a communal level? Couldn't you turn the idea of renunciation in the direction of stewardship? The purpose of every gift is that we might return it. We're called on by the Creator to be good stewards of what's been given. The question, then, is how economically and communally to make it possible for those around us to enjoy what's been given. While that question is very much a personal one, aren't there many important ways in which we should be asking We questions, rather than I questions? My ability to enjoy is in part related to the ability of at least the household of faith and the community of God's people to enjoy. So renunciation is not just a narrow personal challenge. Couldn't one make the argument that renunciation is part of the meaning of enjoyment?"

Meilaender wasn't sure he had any general rules to offer. "It's not that I haven't got any sense that certain rules, such as tithing, might be useful. But there really are different ways of entering the dialectic of renunciation and enjoyment, and they can't be applied very generally. I want to leave room for the individual calling." There might not be any clear general rules, but there is a simple rule that governs the individual approach to possessions: "If my entry into that movement of renunciation and enjoyment doesn't in any way hurt, I probably haven't seriously entered into it. If the renunciation doesn't ask of me anything I'd rather not have asked of me, it's not clear that I've made it into that movement seriously. So there is something subjective about it, but I don't see why that should get us past the notion that there are all sorts of things that we could do without and perhaps ought to do without on some occasion."

Meilaender went on to say that Skillen's effort to integrate renunciation and enjoyment in a social vision of stewardship was "much too serious a view," the product of a "lingering Calvinism. Let renunciation really be renunciation and enjoyment really be enjoyment. Don't tell me that virtue is its own reward. That's fine if you want a Kantian Christianity. Heaven will really be a reward and it will be fun. The purpose of every gift is not simply that it be offered back; it is that it be enjoyed and delighted in. I don't wish to deny the importance of stewardship language, but if I'm right that it's this movement between renunciation and enjoyment that's important, then both must really be acknowledged in some way and not just subtly turned into a form of the other."

Walter Block thought Meilaender was taking much too negative a view of possessions and our attachment to them. "I don't think that you have to be a fallen creature to want to save for a rainy day. It seems to be just prudence not to fritter things away." Block suggested further than the tendency to store things up was not a sign of sin but rather an aspect of human creativity and part of the human capacity to produce wealth. Block also detected in Meilaender's call for renunciation a kind of "zero-sum" thinking about wealth—the idea that if I have more than I need I am thereby preventing someone else from having enough. This is not the way the world works, Block maintained.

But Meilaender was unwilling to grant that the gap between economic and moral life can be closed up that way. "You say it just seems prudent to save up. But what seems natural to human beings who inhabit a fallen world is not necessarily natural in the sense of what a human being would do if his nature had grown to its fruition and really become what it ought to be." Meilaender agreed that zero-sum thinking might not work economically, "but in terms of personal spirituality," he said, "it will certainly work. I can find without much trouble people who can use the things that I have. There is a question, then: What ought I to do about that? This is not a large-scale question about the economics of the world. It is a question of personal spirituality, and it is a mistake to avoid that question by simply translating it back into the large-scale question of political economics. On that question I might not disagree with you terribly. But I'm not willing to let you translate into that language all the time. It's a different question."

Dennis McCann was disturbed by the way Meilaender appeared to be linking prudence to sin. Prudence and efficiency are virtues, he argued, and the need for prudence and efficiency existed prior to the fall. "They are not indications of fallenness but part of the created order, a part of finitude, not sin." This being the case, he suggested that Meilaender had to do more to link the practical requirements of prudence to a spirituality of possessions. Wouldn't it be virtuously prudent, for example, especially in light of Murray's discussion of the importance of self-respect, for someone to save up for his own needs and then disperse everything over and above that to others?

Meilaender allowed that "a kind of prudence would be required by finite conditions, wholly apart from sin." Nevertheless, it would not look like the prudence we associate with rational economic self-interest. "The virtue of prudence is openness to the world, seeing what is really there. It isn't prudential action as we usually understand it. If I really saw what was needed, I would have a present obligation to save for others, and others would have a present obligation to save for my needs. There would be a kind of prudence in an unfallen world, but it would always involve mutuality, exchange, interchange, reciprocity."

In this regard, Meilaender confessed to having trouble with all the talk about self-respect. "I understand that in terms of public policy one ought to take into account how supplying people's needs affects their character. But the Christian ideal is not philanthropic. The philanthropist does not need to be engaged. Whatever love is, it is not modeled on an exchange between individuals who are whole and intact and therefore able to enter into relations with others; it is modeled on an exchange between individuals whose wholeness only comes out of relation."

CLAIMS OF THE POOR

Lawrence Mead reported that he found Meilaender's approach very appealing, but he felt the current religious climate prevents affluent people from undertaking that spiritual pilgrimage. Rich people are denied the freedom to enjoy God's gifts. Hence, theologians like Meilaender have to make it clearer that there is a place for the rich man: he needs to be protected from moral annihilation. "I wish I could approach the problem as you do," he said. "But I hear these clamoring voices that surround me as a rich man. I feel they are saying I have to love others *instead of* myself, not *along with* myself. Within the church, anyway, the poor are sitting in the temple and the rich are their servants. The demands for compensation to the poor are politicized and relentless. Even if I give up my job, if I'm

completely naked, I can't satisfy these people. I'd like to see a theological doctrine that protected me from these extreme claims."

There is no Christian imperative to love oneself, Meilaender responded; there is just a frank recognition that most of us do. The
larger question Mead was raising, Meilaender thought, was how in
the context of Christian thought the poor man should make his
claims. Given that Christians are to renounce at one level their attachment to things, how do they then press their material claims?
"The question really is whether I can make these claims—claims
that might have some basis in justice—in a way that is not just self-
serving, not just an assertion of self."

Not surprisingly, Meilaender found some insight on this point in
Lutheran tradition. "In one of his treatises Luther gives the example
of Samson pulling the pillars down, taking vengeance on his ene-
mies. Luther says Samson's act was wholly impersonal: he simply
understood himself to be God's executor of vengeance. Can the
Christian do that? Luther says it's not impossible, but it's very difficult. You first have to be like Samson, to have the understanding that
it is not your own claims that are at stake but the claims of a human
being who is being treated unjustly. In *Christian Ethics and the City*,
Paul Ramsey considers how the black man might assert his claims
in accordance with the requirement of Christian love, since that sort
of assertion of the self so often seems inappropriate to Christians. He
said it can be done if one is simply holding up the human coun-
tenance before the oppressor, saying 'You cannot do this to *any*
human being.' In a sense it is immaterial that it happens to be
oneself. That's clearly a very hard thing to do. Indeed, human psychology is sufficiently complex that I doubt that anyone ever fully
does it. But thinking about it in this way is a useful tool."

Stokes had suggested earlier that many Americans, in responding to the claims of the poor, are animated by a sense of guilt—an
acute awareness of how much they possess in relation to the rest of
the world. She had found this feeling especially among the college
students with whom she worked. Her remarks prompted a discussion of the uses of guilt.

George Weigel ventured that it is not helpful for students to conclude that because they are eating hamburger other people are
starving. One has to channel this sense of guilt into a systematic
analysis of the causes of poverty.

Indeed, said Neuhaus, one needs to turn a sense of guilt into a
sense of responsibility and a course of action that is actually constructive. "Frequently people feel most guilty about things for
which they are least responsible, which is a kind of guilt posture."

Fleshing out the meaning of responsibility was exactly what Skillen wanted to do in relation to Meilaender's paper, which still seemed to him narrowly focused on the individual spiritual life without sufficient attention to the various spheres of life in which that spirituality gets played out. "I can't get out from underneath what the Calvinists would call the various offices of life, which define the context in which I should be hearing the word of God about being a good steward of possessions and about enjoying them. It's a different kind of responsibility I have relative to my position as a father, as a husband, as a laborer in a particular job, as a member of a particular association, as an American citizen, as a member of a particular local congregation. And eventually we have to ask what the responsibility of business is. What about the structure of public law as it affects the welfare system? What about the structure of families? We have to keep putting ourselves in the boots of the various organizations, associations, and institutions we are addressing. If we don't, we fail to get at the variety of places poverty shows up."

Meilaender said that he suspected there was a "big vision" lurking behind Skillen's remarks, "and I don't have any big vision, just a lot of little visions that may or may not cohere. I'm not opposed to a big vision, though I have a predisposition to believe it isn't possible. Certainly responsibility gets filtered through all those spheres, but I have a tendency to think about them more piecemeal." But if Meilaender resisted a large social vision of responsibility, he did think that the discussion of responsibility and guilt leads, ultimately, to a large religious vision which had not been confronted. "I don't think we push the problem of guilt to its profoundest level. Sometimes people feel guilty for things they really ought not to feel guilty for, and no doubt we do bear guilt for various kinds of neglect which we ought to confess. But there are terrible problems in the world that I'm not particularly responsible or guilty for. That fact, to me, relocates the problem. It helps me see what the real problem is— a very old problem: Why does God permit the world to be as it is? That's the problem for the religious believer. When I say I'm not really guilty because people are starving somewhere, that's not getting me off the hook; it's helping me see the fundamental religious problem: that the God I call unqualifiedly good should nevertheless let there be such a world."

THE MYSTERY OF POVERTY

It is in a sense ironic that the conference should have ended on this note of the mystery of poverty, for the sessions had, after all, begun with some emphatic declarations that poverty in the modern world is no longer a mystery, since we know its origins, and we know, in broad terms, how wealth can be created. But this turn of events in fact reflected the unresolved split between Meilaender's individual pietism on the one hand and the activism of the social analysts (whether to the left or the right) on the other. Not everyone, to be sure, parsed the religious tradition the way Meilaender did. His Lutheran quietism seemed anachronistic to some and clearly ran counter to what he termed the "world-redeeming Calvinism" of others. (To the extent one is concerned with public policy, one is no doubt a world-redeemer of one stripe or another.) Yet many seemed grateful to Meilaender for having refocused attention on the inner movement of the religious struggle to live with possessions and without possessions, to have and not have, to care and not to care— even if it was not exactly clear how one ought to link this struggle to the making of public policy for the poor.

Activism and quietism are not necessarily irreconcilable, of course. Meilaender himself seemed to think one could personally confront poverty as an ineluctable religious mystery while continuing to analyze it as a remediable social problem. But the lively exchanges with Meilaender did suggest that the two attitudes are only rarely brought together and that joining them requires more elasticity of soul than is evident in most religious pronouncements on the poor.

These tensions brought to mind the work of that much heralded but still alien religious figure, Mother Teresa, who has entered rather strenuously into the dialectic of renunciation and enjoyment. Malcolm Muggeridge once put to her the quintessential public policy question: Is what you are doing very efficient? Couldn't government agencies (and here, in light of the conference, he might have added "mediating structures" or "the discipline of the market") accomplish much more for the poor of Calcutta than you and the sisters of the Missionaries of Charity? Mother Teresa's answer was, "The more government agencies do the better; but we are offering the poor something else—Christian love." The more government does, the better—Mother Teresa also approves of doing good at second hand. But the life of faith cannot be lived at second hand. In an era when religious concern for the poor is all too often identified with a particular policy option or prudential judgment, that remains a sobering, and perhaps ultimately illuminating, reminder.

Participants

Dr. Mary Jo Bane
John F. Kennedy School of
    Government
Harvard University

Dr. Robert Benne
Department of Philosophy and
    Religion
Roanoke College

Dr. Brigitte Berger
Sociology Department
Wellesley College

Dr. Walter Block
Centre for the Study of
    Economics and Religion
The Fraser Institute
Vancouver, British Columbia
Canada

Mr. David Heim
The Christian Century

Dr. Robert B. Hill
Consultant-Sociologist
Washington, D.C.

Dr. Kenneth Jameson
Department of Economics
University of Notre Dame

Dr. Leslie Lenkowsky
Institute for Educational Affairs

Rev. Carl W. Lindquist
Sandy Ridge United Methodist
    Church
High Point, North Carolina

Professor Glenn C. Loury
John F. Kennedy School of
    Government
Harvard University

Professor Lawrence H. Mamiya
Department of Religion
Vassar College

Dr. Dennis P. McCann
Department of Religious Studies
DePaul University

Professor Lawrence M. Mead
Department of Politics
New York University

Professor Gilbert Meilaender
Department of Religion
Oberlin College

Mr. Charles A. Murray
Manhattan Institute for Policy
    Research

Mr. Kenneth A. Myers
This World Magazine

Pastor Richard John Neuhaus
The Rockford Institute Center on
    Religion & Society

Mr. Michael Novak
American Enterprise Institute for
    Public Policy Research

Ms. June O'Neill
U.S. Commission on Civil Rights

Dr. Paul E. Sigmund
Department of Politics
Princeton University

Dr. James W. Skillen
Association for Public Justice

Professor Max L. Stackhouse
Andover Newton Theological
    School

Rev. Paul T. Stallsworth
The Rockford Institute Center on
    Religion & Society

Mr. Peter Steinfels
New York Times

Dr. Allison Stokes
Chaplain's Office
Yale University

Mr. George S. Weigel, Jr.
The James Madison Foundation

Mr. Robert L. Woodson
National Center for
    Neighborhood Enterprise